A.P. SINNETT

NATURE'S MYSTERIES

17 essays on Atlantis, Foretelling the future, Palmistry, Miraculous
cures, Occult powers and many other mysteries

CONTENTS

THE TIMELESS WISDOM COLLECTION

Emerson once said: *"Consider what you have in the smallest chosen library. A company of the wisest and wittiest men that could be picked out of all civil countries in a thousand years, have set in best order the results of their learning and wisdom. The men themselves were hid and inaccessible, solitary, impatient of interruptions, fenced by etiquette; but the thought which they did not uncover to their bosom friend is here written out in transparent words to us, the strangers of another age."*

TWC is YOUR small library. Thousands of individual books and anthologies, the best of the best in fiction and non-fiction from the 19th and 20th Centuries, written by men and women whose lives were committed to enlighten the world with the wisdom of the ages.

Our fiction features names as Hemingway, Faulkner, Wells, Orwell, Huxley, Doyle, Twain, Burroughs, Chesterton, Alcott, C. S. Lewis, J. M. Barrie, Edgar Wallace, and hundreds more... Authors who have enriched our lives and forever enlarged our capacity to dream, to get enamored by the characters, to suffer their pain, tragedies, and triumphs as if they were ours; as if they were true...

In self-development and positive-thinking, our authors include Napoleon Hill, Dale Carnegie, Charles Haanel, William Atkinson, Orison Swett Marden, Wallace Wattles, James Allen, Christian D. Larson, Florence Scovell-Shinn, Robert Collier and many more.

In Psychology, we have the works of Freud, Jung, Coué, Coriat, Adler and many others; and in philosophy, the works of Kant, Russell, Whitehead and Eucken, among others. In theosophy and mysticism, our authors include Blavatsky, Bulwer, Besant, Leadbeater, and Sinnett. We feature the works of scientists as Eddington, Darwin, and J. W. Dunne; successful industrialists as Henry Ford, Andrew Carnegie and Charles Schwab; and Economists as John Maynard Keynes...

Thousands of carefully selected masterpieces that have brilliantly captured the essence of life, are now being placed in your hands. *The results of the learning and wisdom of the greatest minds, set in best order,* as Emerson would say. Books for enlightenment, learning, illumination... that will provide the seeker –the one who is ready and is paying attention–, some of the deepest answers to life.

Mauricio Chaves-Mesén, Author of
12 Laws of Successful Entrepreneurs;
Think Success, **and** The Knights of Nostradamus

PREFACE.

This volume reproduces, with some modifications, a series of articles contributed during the last few months to the Sun' and republished in this form with the kind consent of the proprietors of that paper. 'My purpose has been to show readers unaccustomed to the study of what is, commonly called "occult" science, how naturally the investigation of Nature's Mysteries along the lines of recognised scientific research, leads to, and blends with, that farther-reaching research which carries the inquirer beyond the limits of the physically manifested world. For this reason I began by picking up some threads of relatively familiar knowledge concerning the physical world, with the hope of showing how the deeper speculations of physics conduct the thinker, by imperceptible, degrees and without any break of gauge, so to speak, to the regions of superphysical mystery, sometimes erroneously supposed to be permanently shut off from the approach of incarnate intelligence.

Once across the intangible frontier, I have found so much to describe that I have not dealt, in the later articles, which become the chapters' of the present volume, with any other than the varied problems arising in connection with that kind of science which, until it grows more familiar to the cultivated classes generally, will be called "occult"

Introduction

I have endeavoured, turning from one branch of such natural mystery to another, without attempting in any case to compile complete treatises of each, to give the' reader a comprehensive glance of the wide domain of inquiry which lies before the scientific students of the future. As yet I freely grant that none of the branches of 'Superphysical research dealt with in these pages have been truly formulated into sciences. The astrologer, the palmist, the mesmerist, who talk of the " sciences they deal with, are so far misusing the term, because our knowledge of the laws lying behind these pursuits is too imperfect as yet to be described as scientific. But, on the other hand, the persons who do describe them are by no means so deeply in error as the blind and more or less stupid exponents of nineteenth-century prejudice who describe them as folly, imposture, or superstition. Whoever honestly investigates any of these irregular, inchoate sciences will soon be convinced that, however ill we may as yet understand the laws at work, there is a body of natural law with which each is related — bodies of law which, when better understood, will no doubt be often found to blend one into another, and which, in time, will be sufficiently cleared from the mists which still enshroud them, as to be embraced within the recognised scope of such organisations as the Royal Society and the British Association. The more advanced explorers will then be diving in to' mysteries of which the Occultists of our generation are hardly so far cognisant, and in their turn will be ignored by the orthodoxy of the period as not worth the attention of serious men concerned with the practical certainties, as they will then be regarded, of clairvoyant research and astral records. •

Meanwhile there is no hurry in connection with the evolution of human intelligence, and for each of us at present concerned with pursuits that win us more popular contempt than fame, the' time will come when these early lives of conflict with prevailing incredulity will be very amusing in the retrospect. It is difficult to convey to people, for whom the consciousness of other planes', the programme of future lives, and the drift of evolution are empty phrases relating to what for them seems a black and impenetrable curtain of ignorance, how differently the current conditions of any given life are regarded by those who have come into possession of definite knowledge concerning the continuous life of the soul, and the continuity of our relations with the earthly theatre of our progress as well. But whoever attains, in greater or less degree, to a realisation of all this, finds it his business to help on others, so far as lie is able, towards a comprehension thereof, and so books like this before me come to be written not in the expectation that they will sweep away prejudice or enlighten the ignorance of the world at large to any great extent, but for the service of the readers — sufficiently numerous to be very well worth working for already, though few relatively to the population of the civilised world as things stand just now — whose eyes may be opened, to some extent, by familiarity with the realities lying behind various pursuits and inquiries so unfashionable with the multitude.

CHAPTER I. Achievements and Limitations of Science

People who may not be inclined or able to make a special study of science are apt to credit those who are recognised as men of science with knowing a great deal more than they would claim, as knowledge for themselves. The non-scientific person may entirely underrate the delicacy and minute precision of scientific work, but he is apt to overrate its grasp and scope. A correct appreciation of the beauty and magnitude of scientific achievement in one direction, and of the limitations that confront it in another, is very desirable on the part of anyone who, in a general way, is disposed to pay attention to the progress of invention, discovery and research.

To show plainly what I mean by a definite example, I may point to what is known and what is not known about electricity. The extent to which students in that branch of science can now manipulate electricity is wonderful and splendid. We can make electric currents do almost any kind of work we care to set before them. We can make them carry messages or passengers; we can employ them to light houses and streets, or to cook dinners; we can teach them to drive machinery, or to ring bells, and we can all the while measure their energies and quantities as accurately as though we were dealing with so much water or coals. Yet no man of science can tell us the first word of the answer to the question. What is electricity?

We can find out the rate at which electric impulses travel, and we know that this is identical with the speed of light, 186,000 miles a second. We know that currents differ very greatly among themselves in character, some being sharp and intense, and some bulky and feeble. We invent names for these attributes, and call the intensity "volt," and the volume "ampere," and then we go on to invent other names that relate to the different characters of different substances as conductors of electricity, and talk about "ohms" as measuring the resistance such substances oppose to the passage of electric currents; but all the while no one knows whether there is anything at all to be conducted, whether electricity is a fluid, like a gas, only much finer, or a mere vibration in that mysterious medium which pervades all space - the ether.

One might take other illustrations of the idea I want to enforce. We have all known since Newton's time a good deal about the way in which gravitation acts. Many accepted rules guide its invariable behaviour. It is a force that always bears a definite relation to the "mass" (for practical purposes, let us say the weight) of the bodies it affects, and to their distance from one another. But there the knowledge of the most advanced men of science stops short. No one can say a word then asked, What is gravitation? So again with the simplest experiences of everyday life. When you burn a lump of coal, what happens? We know that the various constituents of the coal enter into chemical combination with the oxygen of the atmosphere, but we do not in the least degree know why that process should involve the development of light and heat. Combustion is the commonest, and yet, in some of its aspects, still amongst the most puzzling, phenomena of Nature.

Certainly, in saying this, I do not want to decry the achievements of science, nor even its methods, though these will probably undergo considerable modifications as time goes on; but it is important, in connection with the study of Nature, to realize both the range and limitations of science, because we are in presence of other attempts to investigate Nature besides those of the laboratory and observatory, and I shall have something to say, from time to time, about these, as well as about the achievements or ordinary science along the old familiar road. That which is commonly called science is exclusively "physical" science. It works with instruments made of metal, glass and so on, and has accomplished work that may be fairy termed sublime in its examination of what I will venture to call the outsides of things, but it always stops short in groping after a comprehension of their innermost essence.

Its failures are most obvious when we deal with any of the mysteries of Nature that are associated with life. The extent and minute precision of scientific knowledge concerning the mechanism of the human body are marvellous and admirable. Physiologists have found out all about the processes by which the human body is developed, from the earliest stages of conception to the latest maturity of growth. We know how the muscles that move the body are themselves controlled by the nerves; how these are animated by energies proceeding from the brain; and we even know how some nerves convey orders, so to speak, from the brain to the muscles, and others report sensations from any part of the body to the brain.

We even know what parts of the brain are concerned with the movements of each limb, what parts do business with the interior functions of the body, like digestion or blood circulation, and so forth; and if a man is afflicted with paralysis of some particular limb or muscle, we know exactly where to look for the injury to the brain that may have accounted for the defect. But with all this we have not got one step nearer comprehending the difference between the dead body and the living one.

We have not even got one step towards comprehending the difference between the smallest living weed and its dead companion. Or, at all events, physical science has not accomplished one step in any such direction. Mysteries of that kind lie outside the domain of physical science. Workers in that field are no more to be blamed for not penetrating the mysteries of life than a painter of pictures is to be blamed for not understanding how to make a watch.

Enquiries concerning life and consciousness belong to the domain of what may be called super-physical science, and that, as far as the modern world is concerned at any rate, is a young branch of science still at the stage of observing facts or phenomena which it does not yet fully appreciate. Its conclusions are, so far, little better very often than guesses. Its theories are as yet vague and cloudy in their outlines. Still, it is a progressive branch of science, and is growing up by degrees.

It is possible so to influence the body of a person peculiarly organised - specially sensitive - that the soulmainspring, is set free from it for a time and can act independently of it - can be conscious independently of it, which is the all-important point to be considered. Meanwhile, the body is not conscious. You can prick it with needles and it does not feel, give it ammonia to smell and it does not cough - indeed, more reckless experiments have been tried on persons in the mesmeric state, and their flesh may be burned without their feeling anything; but such experiments as that are deeply to be condemned, because the body is thus injured, even though it does not feel pain at the time, so that when the soul comes back it finds its tenement out of repair.

A result of huge importance is reached by such experiments - equally well reached by those which are innocent as by those which are blameworthy - namely, that the mainspring of the human creature is a separable something which can exist in full consciousness apart from the body, and, when apart from the body, is quite indifferent as to what happens to its deserted tenement. In short, the survival of the soul of a man, after what is commonly called his death, is all but demonstrable by means of mesmeric experiments - not yet, I must confess, within the reach of everyone who would like to try them, any more than the Lick telescope is within the reach of everyone who would like to look through it, but nevertheless within the reach of special enquirers in that line fortunately situated in various ways; and their work has been duly recorded for the advantage of all who are willing to become students of their department of science second-hand. After all, every student in any department of science has to be content with second-hand knowledge of about nineteen-twentieths of all the facts he works with.

In connection with the whole volume of research that goes by the name of Spiritualism, it is as certain as the occasional appearance of comets in the sky, that spiritual *séances* are sometimes - very often - attended by invisible beings who are actually the departed souls of people who once lived in the body. Persons who deny that are as ignorant as they are silly. They are ignorant of the fact that scores - hundreds, indeed - of highly-cultured people bear testimony to their experience in that matter, and they are silly in supposing that their trumpery little prepossessions as to what is probable and what is improbable are to be set against the positive evidence of others at variance with those prepossessions. Also they are marvellously silly in supposing that because they may go to some spiritualistic *séance* and see reason to think the proceedings are imposture, therefore the proceedings at all other *séances* must be imposture too. There are forged bank-notes in the world, no doubt, but that does not militate against the fact that there are also others which are genuine. But, on the other hand, while the rank disbelievers in spiritualism are foolish to an exasperating degree, the devotees of that pursuit are grievously unscientific in their methods as a rule. They are on the threshold of a mighty science, but they too often think themselves in possession of advanced knowledge.

Spiritualism has certainly shown, what, indeed, could have been ascertained in other ways, that the human soul survives the death of the body. But it has not explained the destinies of the human soul after death, because people who pass away only learn about these by degrees, and while they are in a position to communicate with friends still in the flesh, they have rarely gone very far on their ultimate journey, and have not acquired any knowledge concerning its later stages.

A new impulse has been given to scientific thought within the last few years by the discovery and examination of that wonderfully interesting substance, Radium. Formerly it was supposed that an atom of any one of the many substances known as the chemical elements was a definite, indivisible unity. Now we know that all such "atoms" (the word is no longer appropriate in its literal meaning) are a complicated structure built up of far more minute atoms, the nature of which is still under investigation.

Now, I want to convey an idea to begin with as to how small the atom of the chemical elements may probably be. Great mathematicians like Lord Kelvin have worked at this problem, and they come to fairly similar conclusions. Lord Kelvin somewhere illustrates the conclusion by saying that if a drop of water were magnified till it became the size of the earth - all the atoms of which it is composed being magnified in the same proportion - then the atoms would be probably smaller than cricket balls, but larger than small shot. Something between those two sizes!

That suggestion helps the imagination, but we only dazzle it if we talk of the figures concerned. The gases that compose the air we breathe consist, of course, of atoms. In a cubic centimetre of air (a centimetre is a little less than half an inch) there are thirty trillions of gaseous atoms. A trillion is a million billion, and billion is a million million. Now a million alone is a number almost beyond the reach of imagination. If you begin at six o'clock on Monday morning to count seconds, and kept on day and night without a moment's intermission till Saturday evening at six o'clock, you would only have counted half a million seconds, not quite that. And yet, in a little quantity of air, such as you take in hundreds at a breath, there are millions of millions of millions of atoms.

Now about those things which are smaller than chemical atoms. They are radiated or thrown off from the electrical apparatus which generates the much-talked-of Röntgen ray.

Synthetic Matter

Some of us have recently been interested in current statements concerning a new process for the preparation of "synthetic milk" - from vegetable materials - identical in chemical composition with the milk supplied by the cow. A still more remarkable achievement has since been announced - the production of matter itself by a synthetic process dealing with the fundamental etheric atom, which, as occult students have long been aware, though science has but recently caught them up, is the basis of all physical manifestation. Sir William Ramsay, who has been conspicuous in advancing scientific knowledge in reference to the possibility of transmuting one form of physical matter into another, has again been successful in showing that some simple forms of matter can be produced - one might almost say created - by the treatment of the ultimate atom itself, hitherto beyond the range of physical investigation.

This new development of scientific knowledge may be described as beginning with the examination of that highly interesting substance, radium. Some time ago Sir William Ramsay showed that it was possible to obtain helium - a gas previously regarded as an elementary body - from radium. Occult students were not surprised. Radium is a substance of very high atomic weight. That is to say, its atom is composed of a very great number of primary etheric atoms held together in less stable equilibrium than the corresponding condition of similar bodies. That which is described as its radio-activity, is really its readiness to break up into the etheric condition. The Beta particles it throws off in such enormous volume - called at present "electrons" by the ordinary scientist - are really the etheric atoms of which it is built up. Ordinary scientists are for the moment working with an erroneous hypothesis to the effect that these are actually atoms of electricity. They are in reality etheric atoms carrying a definite charge of electricity. To a great extent they stream out in individual atoms (as electrons), but in some cases they break off so to speak in lumps, and when these represent aggregations of atoms equal in number with the aggregations forming definite (so called) elementary bodies, they present themselves in that capacity. That is the way in which Sir William Ramsay obtained his helium, and established the theoretical possibility of

transmutation, thus no longer regarded as a superstition of the misguided alchemist. Following up his first discovery Sir William has since maintained that he has been able to obtain lithium from copper (in other words to transmute copper into lithium), and carbon from silicon. His scientific contemporaries for the most part remain incredulous as regards these achievements, but there is no particular reason why the occultist should distrust the claim.

The latest work done in this department of investigation approaches the problem from the other end of the scale. Instead of breaking up a body of high atomic weight, the attempt now has been to construct bodies of light atomic weight by combining the fundamental etheric atoms.

To explain the method adopted we must remember first of all what goes on in a Röntgen or X-Ray tube. The electrical current projected through such tubes is partially reflected out in the form of Röntgen rays, but also affects the ether in the tube generally. That has been going on ever since Röntgen rays have been studied, but the consequence has only just been realized. That which has now been discovered is that from the glass of an old Röntgen tube it is possible to obtain helium. There was no helium there to begin with. It is assumed that during the flow of the electric current the helium was formed by the aggregation of the etheric atoms or electrons. I need not attempt to describe the precise chemical process by which the helium is set free from the glass. That belongs to the region of technicality, but is not the point in dispute among chemists. The argument of the incredulous opponents of the new discovery is to the effect that as helium exists in the atmosphere it may be have been occluded in the glass to begin with. The answer to this objection is that the quantities obtained by the process described are far in excess of those which could be accounted for in that way. The quantities normally in the atmosphere are infinitesimal.

The present research has been carried on by other distinguished chemists besides Sir William Ramsay - by Professor Collie and Mr. Patterson - and these investigators have obtained the rare gas, neon, from tubes that have been filled in the first instance with hydrogen (of course in a highly rarefied condition).

There is nothing surprising in the results from the point of view of the occult student, and they may be looked upon as the thin end of a wedge that will ultimately be driven much further into old-fashioned conceptions relating to the constitution of matter. The amusing feature of the present controversy, as it is going on in the scientific world while we write, is that no attention whatever is paid, in that world, to the fact that the whole volume of knowledge towards which these investigations are groping their way, was anticipated by occult investigations in the year 1895, when in the November number of the magazine then called *Lucifer* the atomic constitution of hydrogen, oxygen and some other bodies, was fully set forth in much greater detail than later scientific investigation has yet reached. Clairvoyant research showed not merely that these bodies were composed of etheric atoms, but actually detected their number and arrangement within the hydrogen, oxygen and other atoms. The hydrogen atom consists of eighteen etheric atoms and this is a key number, giving us the number of etheric atoms in any (hitherto called) elementary body of high atomic weight. Disregarding this discovery with sublime indifference, the modern physicist is speculating wildly on the question how many "electrons" go to the composition of hydrogen, and Sir Joseph Thompson in a recent lecture suggested 1,700 as a probable number, guided apparently by the entirely delusive idea that the number would be indicated by the ratio of the mass of the hydrogen atom to the mass of the electron. The atom of any given physical body is a solar system in miniature, the negative etheric atoms representing the planets, and perhaps a positively electrified "atom" of some unknown matter, the sun of the system. Occult knowledge concerning the beautiful phenomena of Nature dribbles out to us by degrees and we are not yet in a position to say much about the nature of positive electricity. The scientific world is busy with its investigation, but does not seem yet to be on anything like the right trail. Meanwhile at all events Sir William Ramsay's synthetic helium is a very promising addition to the armoury of weapons with which the deeper mysteries of matter will be attacked at a later date.

Thus it has come to pass that some mysteries of Nature scouted and hooted at fifty years ago as empty pretences of fraud and imposture, are already recognized as worthy of serious attention.

Others, of which the importance has not yet been generally allowed, will establish their claims in due time. Mesmerism, for example, which was ridiculed in the middle of the past century as though it were nonsense and superstition, is acknowledged on all hands now to be a fact in Nature, though few people understand it properly as yet, except those who have been at work with it for many years. So with what is called "thought-transference," the power some people have, if they are specially gifted in that direction, of becoming aware, without being told in any ordinary way, of what some other person is thinking.

Mathematics and indirect experiment may enable us to find out the size of the water molecule, but we shall never see it with any physical instrument. But such things can be seen by the "clairvoyant" faculty of persons peculiarly gifted. As the human race improves, such people will become more numerous than they are at present, but already they are numerous enough to enable students of "occult' science to be quite sure of their existence, and to compare their observations one with another.

That phrase, by the way, "occult," merely means something extra-mysterious for the time being. The few people who possessed some knowledge of electricity in the days of ancient Egypt would have called that occult science. A few generations hence there will be nothing occult about thought-transference, or clairvoyance, but, for the moment, the laws governing those faculties are still hidden from us to so great an extent, that the study of such matters lies still in the department of occult science.

The term "clairvoyance" means, of course, no more than clear seeing - seeing, that is to say, with the eye of the mind, in some mysterious fashion, which has nothing to do with optics, but, nevertheless, is a *bona-fide* perception of actual things. Clairvoyance is a faculty as old as the world. There are perfectly well-authenticated stories about it in ancient history, but no evidence of that sort will make people believe what they do not want to believe, so I will come to more recent investigations. One of the most patient and careful investigators who have written on this subject is Dr Gregory, author of a book called *Animal Magnetism*, published in the middle of the last century. He was lucky enough to meet with a good many people who were endowed with the necessary faculties, and willing to let him experiment with them. In his day it seems to have been taken for granted that clairvoyance was a faculty that could only be exercised when people were in the mesmeric state, so all Dr Gregory's subjects were first mesmerized, and then employed to look at things that could not be seen with their physical eyes.

For example, he would get a bagful of nuts, each made up for children's parties, with a printed motto inside. Anyone present would take one of these nuts out of the bag at random. It would be given to the "sensitive," or clairvoyant, and he (or she) would read the motto, or, anyhow, tell correctly what it was. Then, before everyone present, the nut would be cracked, and the clairvoyant reading verified. These demonstrations were very neat and satisfactory, because they precluded the possibility that the motto could be read by thought-transference. Nobody present knew what any particular nut contained.

Many French experimentalists in the middle of the century entangled their researches with attempts to foresee the future by help of clairvoyance. It does not follow that because a peculiarly gifted person may be able to see what *is* at a distance in space, he may be able to see what only *may be* at a distance in time. All the same, a great deal of interesting information on the subject of true clairvoyance is to be found in the French literature of mesmerism; and though we do not understand much yet about the laws which govern the exercise of this faculty, everyone who has the patience to become, in even a moderate degree, a student of occult science, knows that such a faculty exists.

We shall never see an atom of carbon or oxygen by means of microscopes, but we shall be able to examine their structure and composition by means of clairvoyant faculties turned in that direction, for size is no embarrassment to the eyes of the mind. The smallest things in Nature are as visible to that sense as the medium-sized things that suit our common eyesight, and the clairvoyant sight can be no more embarrassed by the magnitude in the other direction. Astronomical distances are as well within its focus as those which we can measure with our hands.

CHAPTER II. Some Higher Faculties of Consciousness.

Some mysteries of Nature that were scouted and hooted at fifty years ago as the empty pretences of fraud and imposture, are already recognised as realities and worthy of serious attention. Others, of which the importance has not yet been generally allowed, will establish their claims in due time. Mesmerism, for example, which was ridiculed in the middle of the past century as though it were nonsense and superstition, is acknowledged on all hands now to be a fact in Nature, though few people understand it properly as yet, except those who have been at work with it for many years. So with what is called "thought-transference," the power some people have, if they are specially gifted in that direction, of becoming aware, without being told in any ordinary way, of what some other person is thinking.

That used to be ridiculed as nonsense by orthodox scientific people until the Society for Psychical Research carried out such a long series of experiments on the subject, and obtained such conclusive results, that now, if anyone says he does not believe in thought-transference, he merely shows his ignorance of established truth. A great many other branches of inquiry hitherto carried on by the irregular auxiliaries of science will gradually come within the area of recognised work. Of that we may feel sure, because enough Some Higher Faculties of Consciousness has been learned about Nature already to show that it is rich in mysteries that never can be investigated by means of instruments in a laboratory. Thera 'are' forces far too subtle to influence galvanometers and electroscopes, which are, nevertheless, susceptible of investigation, if specially gifted people use their inborn faculties in the right way.

I shall come back directly to show how some such faculties have been employed to anticipate Professor Thompson's discovery of bodies smaller than atoms, but it will be as well to describe first what kind of faculty has been used (incidentally, among other uses) for that purpose. All possible methods of investigating the mysteries of Nature may be divided up into "two great groups: the physical methods and the superphysical methods. That is to say, we may use microscopes, telescopes, spectroscopes, and all the other instruments that can be made by the optician, or we may use abnormal, unusual, human faculties. Of course, where they can be employed, the physical instruments are much the more convenient, but they are limited in their range. Think of a microscope, for example. With the best that can be made you can see the minute bacteria of disease about which so much is said in the present day. Some of their germ cells are no more than 1/5000th of an inch in diameter. You can see them in a good microscope, but one of them would be an elephant compared to one of the molecules or atoms that make up a drop of water.

Mathematics and indirect experiment may enable us to find out the size of the water molecule, but we shall never see it with any physical instrument. But such things can be seen by the " clairvoyant " faculty of persons peculiarly gifted. As the human race improves, such people will become more numerous than they are at present, but already they are numerous enough to enable students of " occult " science to be sure of their existence, and to compare their observations one with another.

That phrase by the-way, "occult," merely means something extra-mysterious for the time being. The few people who possessed some knowledge of electricity in the days of ancient Egypt would have called that occult science. A few generations hence there will be nothing occult about thought-transference, or clairvoyance, but, for the moment, the laws governing those faculties are still hidden from us to so great an extent, that the study of such matters lies still in the department of occult science.

The phrase "clairvoyance" means, of course, no more than clear seeing-seeing, that is to say, with the eyes of the mind, in some mysterious fashion, which has nothing to do with optics, but, nevertheless, is a fine perception of actual things. The idea was so strange to the early inquirers who first dropped upon it, that they may well have been excused for thinking it supernatural. And people in the present day who are still under the influence of the thinking which prevailed in the scientific world fifty years ago, do not believe in the supernatural, so they put aside all they could face to hear about clairvoyance as so much humbug and nonsense. But they might as well put aside the Transvaal War as humbug and nonsense, on the ground that they have not taken part in it. Certainly I do not want them to change their habits of mind so far as to believe in the "supernatural."

There cannot be any such thing, because whatever is, comes within the domain of Nature.

But the truth of the matter is, that a vast variety of things, of which nobody as yet suspects the existence, come within that domain, and as we make acquaintance with them one by one, each at the first glance looks so unfamiliar that we think it must be fraud, nonsense, hallucination. Clairvoyance is a faculty as old as the world. There are perfectly well authenticated stories about it in ancient history, but no evidence of that sort will make people believe what they do not want to believe, so I will come to more recent investigations. One of the most patient and careful investigators who have written on' this subject is Dr Gregory, author of a book called Animal Magnetism published in the middle of the century. He was lucky enough to meet with a good many people who were endowed with the necessary faculties, and willing to let him experiment with them. In his day it seems to have been taken for granted that clairvoyance was a faculty that could only be exercised when people were in the mesmeric state, so all Dr Gregory's subjects were first mesmerised, and then employed to look at things that could not be seen with their physical eyes.

For example, he would get a bagful of nuts, each made up for children's parties, with a printed motto inside. Anyone present would take one of these nuts out of the bag at random. It would be given to the " sensitive," or clairvoyant, and he (or she) would read the motto, or, anyhow, tell correctly what it was. Then, before everyone present, the nut would be cracked, and the clairvoyant reading verified. These demonstrations were very satisfactory, because they precluded the possibility that the motto could be read by thought-transference. Nobody present knew what any particular nut contained.

Many French experimentalists in the middle of the century entangled their researches with attempts to foresee the future by help of clairvoyance. It does not follow that because a peculiarly-gifted person may be able to see what is at a distance in space, he may be able to see what only may be at a distance in time. All the same, a great deal of interesting information on the subject of true clairvoyance is to be found in the French literature of mesmerism; and though we do not understand much yet about the laws which govern the exercise of this faculty, everyone who has the patience to become, in even a moderate degree, a student of occult science, knows that such a faculty exists Without stopping now, however, to relate personal experiences, I want to explain that clairvoyance is the power by means of which our comprehension of the innermost minutiae of Nature will ultimately be extended far beyond the limits set by the imperfections of physical instruments.

We shall never see an atom of carbon or oxygen by means of microscopes, but we shall be able to examine their structure and composition by means of clairvoyant faculties turned in that direction, for size is no embarrassment to the eyes of the mind. The smallest things in Nature are as visible to that sense as the medium-sized things that suit our common eyesight, and the clairvoyant sight can be no more embarrassed by magnitude in the other direction. Astronomical distances are as well within its focus as those which we can measure with our hands.

CHAPTER III. The Age of the World.

" My friends," said a simple-minded preacher once in the hearing of one of my friend's, "this world is very old. It is six thousand years old!" Of course, the good man thought he had Scriptural assurance in support of that estimate; but the progress of knowledge has induced us, not to treat Scriptural statements with disrespect, but to read them in a new way, and thus all educated people in the present age are well aware that the planet on which we live has been slowly brought to its present degree of perfection during a great many millions of years, and 'that the six thousand of our primitive ancestral belief is rather a phase of the present time than a period that can be treated, in any comprehensive sense, as the past.

On the other hand, though we all know that geological evidence not only proves the enormous antiquity of the earth, but makes it certain that man existed upon it many millions of years ago (human skulls having been found in strata that must have been formed as long ago as that), we have no direct literary evidence of human activity extending further back than a few thousand years before Christ.

European records are all very recent. Those of Egypt go back much further, but the dates to which we assign the earliest buildings, sculpture, and inscriptions are, to a great extent, matters of speculation. A fragment of an old Egyptian history, the bulk of which has been lost, gives us a catalogue of kings and dynasties covering a period that has been variously estimated at from 3500 to 5000 years before Christ; but everyone admits that remains apparently associated with the earliest part of this period are of a kind that must have been preceded by long ages of civilisation. The tendency of archaeologists, however, has been to ignore what cannot be demonstrated, so students of this subject have, for the most part, drifted into the habit of assuming that civilisation on earth began with the known beginnings of Egyptian civilisation, and that if we go back behind 5000 b.c., we have to think of mankind as in a savage condition. The men who lived millions of years ago, and whose skulls and flint implements are to be found in geological deposits that cannot have a less antiquity than that, are generally thought of as a mere primitive race living in caves and unacquainted with the use of metals.

None the less does every fresh discovery or legitimate inference tend to bring a larger allowance of past ages into continuous relation with the historic period. Professor Flineffs Petrie, who has done a great deal of patient work in Egypt, and has lately given a course of lectures at the Royal Institution on the prehistoric remains he has discovered, helps himself to another two thousand years, more or less, to account for their existence. The things themselves — pottery, flint implements, and sculpture — do not afford any clue to the date at which they were made, but Professor Petrie thinks that the known rate at which the River Nile deposits mud, does afford such a clue. Egypt, as an inhabited country, is the creation of the River Nile. Its cultivatable soil has been spread over the bed rock by the inundations of a vast series of ages, and if you measure the depth of the deposit, you get a time limit within which every phase Egyptian Existence must have been included. Thus, 7000 years before Christ seems him the limit within which the complete history of Egypt must be compressed. I propose to show reason why we need not submit to those narrow limits in considering the past civilisation of Egypt, and why it is desirable to attack the problem in quite a different way from that adopted by Professor Petrie, if we set out in search of general conclusions concerning the antiquity of civilised mankind on earth, irrespective of any particular area within which such civilisation may, at any given period, have fermented.

Whenever this investigation is seriously undertaken by the scientific world, it must turn round the great problem of Atlantis. I have said that we have no literary records concerning the remote past but that remark may be qualified. We have none that are as yet universally accepted as trustworthy, but Plato has left us some account, flavoured, it is true, with obviously fabulous details, concerning the existence, at a period long anterior to the earliest known dynasties of the 'Egyptian catalogue, of a great island or continent situated in the middle of what is now the Atlantic Ocean. He got his information from Egyptian priests. Till recently the whole story was treated as a fable, but modern research has gone far, by ordinary methods, to establish the fact that such a continent as he describes did really exist at one time. Of course, there is nothing at variance with accepted scientific views in that belief.

Geologists freely admit the broad principle that most of the land which is dry at the present time was once under sea water, and presumably, therefore, that a great deal of the present ocean bed was once dry land. At the Edinburgh meeting of the British Association, Professor Lapworth spoke of the " secular undulations of the earth's crust," which alternately, in periods of unknown duration, changed the whole face of geography. The only reason why the existence of Atlantis is not universally recognised is that, as yet, we are not supposed to have sufficient proof of its existence. So far, only some students of the subject think the proof, along ordinary lines, sufficient and complete. Some of the scientific men connected with the ocean surveys of the Challenger are disposed to regard the configuration" of the Atlantic bed as fully establishing the Atlantis theory.

Donnelly, the American writer, brings forward a mass of testimony to show that the ancient beliefs, the artistic work, and the natural phenomena — the plants and animals — of Mexico and the Mediterranean basin had a common origin, which could only have been possible if at one time those parts of the world were in touch with each other along land communications, instead of being separated by great expanses of ocean as they are now. And since Donnelly wrote his book, some overwhelming testimony has been forthcoming to confirm the Atlantean story. But before I come to that, it will be convenient to describe how it comes to pass that students of occult science have rushed on enormously in advance of investigation along commonplace channels of research, in reference to the conditions of the world's civilisation at the time when Atlantis was in full life and vigour.

The faculty of clairvoyance, of which I have already spoken in reference to the power it gives to some of its most gifted exponents of examining the structure of atoms far too small for any microscopic investigation, is equally applicable to the investigation of the world's history in long past ages.

A time will most certainly come when this wonderful power will be recognised as the most potent instrument of research which science can employ. As yet it is exercised in perfection by only a few persons known to me, but within the Theosophical connection there are several sufficiently endowed and developed— for the faculty requires not merely a natural gift, but great perseverance and devotion to the task, for its effective culture — to provide for the comparison of observations one with another, to eliminate occasional errors, and to fill up detail when the problem in hand has to do with the investigation of some long past period.

In that way the modern devotees of occult science have at last put together such, a mass of information relating to the Atlantean period, that we really know much more about it than, for instance, about the so called historical period of Egyptian civilisation. And we have been made acquainted, in connection with this research, with the actual dates at which great changes in the configuration of the earth's geography have taken place. Ordinary geology, as I have said, makes it certain that such changes have taken place, but it does not tell us when they happened. Clairvoyant research does tell us when the changes occurred, and, more than this, gives us actual maps of the earlier configurations.

"The Story of Atlantis," the results of clairvoyant investigation into that most interesting period the world's history, has been published in a book bearing that title. The whole narrative is too elaborate and fascinating in its interest to be dealt with in detail in this article, which has necessarily been concerned with collateral matters, but I want especially to explain how the knowledge we occult students possess concerning Atlantis clears up questions connected with the early history of Egypt that would be quite unmanageable in any other way.

Knowing how the geographical changes have been going on, we can reconcile the 9000-year limit (reckoning back from the present time), which Professor Petrie assigns to the whole history of Egypt, with the fact, of which in other ways we are quite equally sure, that the grandest civilisation of Egypt was flourishing many tens of thousands of years before the country entered upon that period. That period did not, in real truth, present its growth and development, but merely its gradual decay.

Once upon a time — I will go into more exact detail later — land stretched almost uninterruptedly right across the region which is now the Atlantic Ocean, from the land we now call Mexico — the extreme westerly limit — to the northern shores of what is now Africa (the southern part of Africa had not then as yet come into existence), and so on right across what is now Egypt (there was no Red Sea then) to what is now Asia. The land, in fact, at the time I am speaking of made a huge belt round the earth. There was no North or South America, no Europe, no South Africa. Much later on, through successive changes that I will not stop now to describe, some approximation to the present condition of affairs was reached, but still there existed in the middle of the Atlantic Ocean an island — the remnant of the original vast continent of Atlantis — and this island was about as big in area as all modern Europe, without Persia. The Red Sea had been invented by that time (it was the result of changes that took place about 80,000 years ago), and so matters remained without any great further alteration until about 11,500 years ago.

That was the period during which the grand civilisation of Egypt was actually in progress. Why have its traces not been more definitely identified? Because at the date last mentioned, 11,500 years ago, the latest of the great cataclysmic convulsions that have from time to time altered the configuration of the earth took place. The vast islands constituting the remains of Atlantis subsided with terrific suddenness, and the sea, which then covered what is now the desert of Sahara, was driven eastward so as to completely deluge the land of Egypt. The great pyramid, already in existence (modern archeologist utterly mistaken as to the date of its construction), was for a time under water. Lower Egypt was obliterated as a region of land, and spent a good many years as so much sea-bed. All traces of the old civilisation disappeared except as regards some of the temples, which, like the great pyramid, are really prediluvian, and when the next change took place, which elevated, to some extent, the whole of Northern Africa and shouldered off the waters of the Saharan Sea, leaving that region to dry up and become a desert, then the Nile resumed business a river channel, and set to work to make a new Egypt by the deposition of fresh mud. It is this, its latter-day task, that the modern archaeologist treats as though it had occupied the whole of past time.

And now, having stated what did occur — as occult students ascertain by surer methods than the guesses of archaeology — let me, in conclusion for the present, show how some commonplace testimony of the ordinary kind has lately cropped up to vindicate occult research in reference to the latest period of Atlantean history and the final disappearance of the last remaining island. Mexico, as I have said, has from immense antiquity been habitable land. A French archeologist, Dr Le Plongdon, has been at work there for many years. He has written books about his discoveries, and he has been the first person to decipher the Mexican hieroglyphics (which differ from those of Egypt). In 1893 Mr E. J. Howell, in the course of a lecture before the Society of Arts, recounted the contents of letters he had received from Dr Le Plongeon concerning his then recent work. He had succeeded in translating a certain manuscript known to archaeologists as the Troano MS. It had never before been deciphered, but Le Plongeon found it to contain a straightforward narrative of the submergence of Atlantis. It is in itself an ancient Mexican manuscript of immense antiquity, and it says that the catastrophe took place 8160 years before the writing of this book."' Ten countries, it says, were torn asunder in the convulsion, and sank with their 64,000,000 inhabitants. The date given, it will be seen, fairly well corresponds with that obtained by clairvoyant research, and it is not creditable to the ordinary non-occult students of the bygone history and past evolution of our race, that Le Plongeon's great discovery should, so far, have excited so little attention.

The real, grand, early civilisation of Egypt was introduced by migrations of enterprising colonists from the great Atlantean continent long before the contraction of that continent to the dimensions of the island which lasted till years ago. Everything, in fact, in any part of the ancient world had an

Atlantean origin, just as a few thousand years hence everything then existing about the world in the shape of civilisation will necessarily be recognised as having had a European origin. Nobody can begin to understand the old world, or the beginnings of the civilzation in the midst of which we live, until he has obtained a comprehensive grasp of the state of mankind in the Atlantean period. Atlantis is the key to all knowledge concerning the past history and evolutionary progress of our race; and in the next chapter I propose to go on with this subject, and to show how a rich and varied civilisation spread over large portions of the earth, not merely a few thousand, but even a million, years ago.

CHAPTER IV. The Story of Atlantis.

Among all the investigations that have been undertaken by the students of occult science with the view of enabling us better to understand the world in which we live, few have been more important than that which has presented us with a fairly complete and coherent picture of the civilisation that prevailed on the earth in long past ages, before the slow processes of geological change had fashioned the continents into the shape with which we are now familiar. Apart from the human interest of the story thus unveiled, it puts an entirely new complexion (for those to whom the crudities of mediaeval theology have hitherto stood in the way of truthful conceptions concerning the methods of Divine activity) on the whole theory of creation.

Everyone in these days has been made familiar with the idea of evolution as the method by which higher forms of vegetable and animal life are gradually developed from those which come first in the order of time. But, while we know that biologists require millions of years to account for the evolution of one species of animal from another; most people have been idly content to think of the transition from the primitive savage of the " stone age," as it is vaguely called, to the intellectual perfection that we find developed in ancient Greece, let us say, as accomplished within the one or two thousand years, which are all that our modern historical knowledge provides for the period civilisation anterior to ancient Greece. Millions of years are assigned to the natural processes that are required to differentiate the body of a sheep, let us say, from the body of the preceding animal, whatever that may have been in the order of development; but even professed evolutionists carelessly suppose that the mind of a man is something that can grow up like a mushroom in a relatively brief interval.

The blunder is due to the habit people have got into of looking merely at the outside of things, at the mere physical world around us, without suspecting that that is only one aspect of Nature. It is only the occultist, so far, who realises that the unseen aspects of Nature are themselves the result of a gradual evolution, and that changes of condition in the human soul are as much the result of evolutionary growth as the changes in the condition of its bodily organism. Later on I propose to discuss some of the conditions that regulate growth of that sort — amongst the most fascinating of all the mysteries that are half revealed and half concealed by the outward circumstances of our terrestrial existence: but in all natural study it is well to begin by getting a grasp, as complete as possible, of the facts we have to deal with, putting off till later the broad inferences from these which give us a comprehensive theory of life.

I have shown already how ancient tradition suggests that inhabited land once existed where the Atlantic Ocean now spreads its watery curtain over the past; that ocean soundings tend to confirm that tradition; that the accepted principles of geology are in harmony with it; and that archaeological discoveries in Mexico have gone far to establish it on a foundation of recorded certainty. I may add one little bit of testimony from the experience of a friend who has travelled a great deal in Mexico. At various places about that country, in forests and primaeval wildernesses, traces have been found of an onroad — a solidly-built causeway of stone— which appeared to run from some place in the interior of the country to the seashore that end of the peninsula of Yucatan, beyond the coast line into the islands. On these also traces of the old road have been found, as also in the shallow transparent waters between them and the mainland.

The road is as plain an assurance as though it were a record in writing, that at some former time there was a civilised inhabited region in the direction towards which that road points. The region is under water now, but once upon a time it was to the world at large what Europe is now — the home of the most advanced civilisation of the period. Clairvoyant research has enabled us to recall the general features of that time and ever more — many details of the social, industrial, and scientific characteristics of the time. For let it be understood that there is no limit to the power of clairvoyant research except that which affects the capacity of any given clairvoyant investigator to exercise the power. The memory of Nature, so to speak, is infallible.

I will not stop now to go into the metaphysics of the problem, but there is such a thing as a universal memory, quite independent of that little fragmentary memory enjoyed by each item of the human family, and the highest kind of clairvoyance enables the person who enjoys it to draw upon that universal memory, which is just as clear and certain in reference to events that have transpired a million years ago as to those of yesterday. On that topic alone I could dilate at great length, but our methods of communicating ideas from one to another are such that it is necessary to pay attention to one thing at a time; so, putting off to a more convenient opportunity a fuller exposition of the theory of the higher clairvoyance — of Nature's memory, in fact — I   will go on to relate something of what is remembered concerning Atlantis a million years ago.

The configuration of the earth at that time was such that land stretched in an unbroken, continental mass from what is now Mexico to Scotland. Southward it included the greater part of what is now Brazil, and stretched across to what is now Africa, then sea for the most part, except for its northern portion. This northern portion stretched out a tongue of land, of which the present Canary Islands were the mountain tops, towards the great Atlantean continent, and a narrow strait between its extremity and the Atlantean shore was the only water it would have been necessary to cross in a journey from China to Peru.

The greatest capital of this vast continent, which, of course, included many nations and many great cities, was situated, in what is now mid-ocean, between the Cape de Verde Islands and the West Indies. The condition of things, however, to which I am now referring was not that to which Plato's tradition refers. Stupendous changes came over the scene before the huge continent was reduced in size to the island Atlantis, which existed up to about 11,500 years ago. Of these changes I will speak presently, but let us took back first to the really palmy days of the old Atlantean civilisation.

I take the period of a million years ago, not because that was the beginning of the civilisation in question, but because this was then at its height. It had been the product of a long course of human evolution, the study of which would take us back to an almost immeasurably greater antiquity; but the first conception concerning the past that it is important to get firmly in the mind, is that humanity, in epochs of which modern history has entirely lost sight, was in some respects quite on a level with that of our own day. In others it was far behind, but its deficiencies had reference to its moral rather than to its intellectual development, as will presently be made clear.

At the particular period on which I have focused my attention, the people were innocent enough. They were under the very benign rule of wise and lofty-minded emperors'; and, though the idea of political liberty, as we understand the term, had hardly dawned upon them, they were docile, industrious, &d peaceful, so that there was no extreme poverty amongst them, no fretful discontent. Public institutions were designed for the welfare of all, and life was much smoother all round than with us. The arts and sciences were developed to a high degree. Writing, painting, architecture, and sculpture were all practised as freely as amongst ourselves, and the Engineering work accomplished was on a scale that would almost dazzle the builders of the Forth Bridge or the Nile dam. But it ran, so to speak, in very different channels from our engineering.

Invention had not followed the same lines as in our day, and the very forces employed in engineering work were quite unlike those we manipulate. I do not gather that the Atlanteans had any steam machinery, but, on the other hand, they had control of some natural force that at present we have lost sight of. This was a repulsive force of some kind, the use of which enabled Atlanteans to navigate the air in a way we have not yet been able to imitate. Their air boats emitted an energy that at the same time kept them suspended above the earth's surface, and could be employed to drive them in any required direction.

Their chemistry, again, had advanced along lines on which we, their remote descendants, have not yet succeeded in travelling, and they had got at the secret of transmutation, so that the manufacture of gold — which they prized for its ornamental value quite as much as we do — was a regular branch of industry. In the present day advanced chemists have got beyond the silly stage of denial which characterised the mind of the last century, and every great chemist would now agree that there is nothing absurd in the theory of transmutation, though we have not yet got the clue to the process. Modern accepted views of the constitution of matter point to transmutation as a possibility of the future.

Amongst the achievements of the, Atlanteans, conspicuous by their absence, stands prominently the art of printing. If that simple invention had been hit upon earlier in the world's history, it would have made later progress very different. Inscriptions, even on stone, are evanescent compared to those on printed paper, because you have thousands of the one for every single example of the other. England, with all its museums and buildings, might sink beneath the waves, all Europe might follow its example, but the records of its life could never perish, because they are to be found in every library in the world. In Atlantean times records of civilisation were all concentrated within its own area, and that was limited. Asia was inhabited, certainly, but not by a people comparable in civilisation with the Atlanteans. Their time of progress was to come later, so, when the heyday of Atlantean civilisation was over, when ultimately the very land itself perished, its only traces were found in colonies that for various reasons we can quite understand were very far from repeating the conditions of the parent state.

And amongst the knowledge conspicuous by its absence must be included all that which gives us our power of rapid communication all about the world. There were no electric telegraphs in Atlantean times, and from the Atlantean's point of view there was no world outside his own continent worth talking about. There was plenty of other land about the world. Australia, for instance, was about three or four times as large as it is now, and was incalculably older land than Atlantis, for, going back many millions of years ago, there was a completely different configuration of the world's geography from that of the Atlantean period. But nowhere, except in the Atlantean continent was there any civilisation.

I have explained that, while without some of the scientific acquirements of our own period, the Atlanteans were in possession of other knowledge which we have not yet recovered. Amongst these they exercised some powers that are very faintly, as yet, foreshadowed by the imperfectly understood phenomena of mesmerism. These powers rendered the mere muscular superiority of one person over another quite 'unimportant We may call the power in question " psychic force," for want of a better name. Now, this could be acquired quite as' fully by women as by men. Indeed, the women possessed it, as a rule, in a somewhat higher perfection than the men, and the result was that the relative position of the sexes was by no means the same amongst the Atlanteans as amongst ourselves.

Women were fully the equals of men in effective strength, and, as a consequence, were their equals socially and politically. Not that in those days people exercised political power by voting, as with us, but women were appointed members of various councils that were entrusted with important functions, and were made rulers of provinces under the beneficent despot at the head of things. It is not my province to discuss political questions, or I might launch out into a panegyric of this interesting system.

From the summit level of its happiest age — about a million years ago — Atlantean civilisation began to decline. The innocence of the people was rather the innocence of childhood than that of enlightened spiritual conviction. The powers many of them possessed were easily turned to selfish and ignoble uses. Loyalty to the beneficent rulers began to fade away. Insurrections and rebellions broke out, and by degrees the country became a prey to formidable civil wars. The huge chapters of the world's history which the Atlantean period represented drew towards its melancholy close.

Vast cataclysmic convulsions began to break up the great continent, and about 800,000 years ago changes set in which ultimately rent it in twain, separating it from what then gradually began to grow into what is now America, and breaking off its north-eastern portion. This in time became joined on to new land, formed by the upheaval of Scandinavia and Western Germany, so that, at the close of these great changes, we find a huge body of land stretching from the North Cape down to Spain, and, of course, including the region which is now Great Britain and Ireland. These did not become insular till very much later.

CHAPTER V. The Bequests of Atlantis.

The story told in the last chapter was not merely one of entrancing interest in itself, but important as enabling us to understand the condition of the world as we now find it. I must follow it up a little further in order to give my readers a clue to the comprehension of much that lies around us in the world to-day that would be hopelessly mysterious without that clue.

I have spoken of the degradation, and decay that gradually set in towards the close of the million of years that have elapsed since the old continent was enjoying its maximum glory. But there were some among the Atlanteans more enlightened than the rest, and as the old civilisation has corrupted, these people led great streams of emigration to other parts of the world. One such Stream gave rise to the real early civilisation of Egypt, at that time a vast region with a sea-shore on the west — where now we find nothing but the vacant sands of the Sahara — and a northern portion that stretched right over that which is now the eastern basin of the Mediterranean.

The leaders of this great migration were far superior in knowledge and moral -growth to the people who were then native to the country. From among them were chosen the kings, priests, and teachers of the indigenous population, and at the first glance it does seem surprising that we have no intelligible records left that embody the story of their achievements; but the truth is, that only a small portion of modern Egypt coincides with the original Egypt of the early period. Part of that is under the eastern

Mediterranean, and part under the desert sands; while, as regards the part which did correspond with the present inhabited portion, that was for a prolonged period itself under water, so that the sites of the early cities were entirely obliterated by sedimentary deposits, not to speak of the alluvial deposits of Nile mud which were laid over these again when the country once more, in the progress of ages, became dry land, and when the river draining the African interior resumed something like its former course. Its deflection by only a few miles one way or the other from that former course would be enough to baffle archaeological research, not even guided by the suspicion that there is anything to look for at any great distance from the present course of the stream.

However, in spite of all these confusing circumstances, there is one monument that might link modern research with the great early civilisation if we could only escape from fixed prepossessions as to its origin, and that is the great pyramid itself. This is really a bequest from the very early time. Absurd conjectures of all sorts have gathered round the great pyramid, and Egyptian monarchs of the historical period, who were merely concerned, in reality, with repairing or altering it, have been accepted by Egyptologists as having been its builders. Theorists on a still humbler mental level — and impressed with the notion that the Old Testament must contain the complete history of the ancient world — have supposed that it was built to store the corn produced in the years of plenty against the years of scarcity foretold by Joseph. Other imaginative persons, impressed with the curious relations that undoubtedly exist between the position and dimensions of the pyramid on the one hand, and the facts -of astronomy on the other, have persisted in regarding the strange building as an astronomic observatory for which it has almost every conceivable disqualification.

If I were to attempt an account of the purposes for which it really was erected, I should have to write of nothing else for a long time to come in order to make the narrative even intelligible, and then some of its purposes would remain in obscurity for want of a deeper occult knowledge than I can lay claim to. The time has not yet come for the complete removal of the mystery that enshrouds it, but, anyhow, this much is known to people who have even partial access to the " Memory' of Nature." The pyramid was built, not in the reign of Cheops, or Kufu'as he is called sometimes, 4000 or 5000 years before Christ, but at a period more like 200,000 years ago, under the direction of authorities who foresaw that, in the changes with which geography was threatened, it would for a time lie under water. They wished it to survive any such experience, and for this reason adopted the very stable form we see. Of course, the great majority of the smaller pyramids that stud the Nile valley were of relatively recent date, and actually were designed to be the tombs of kings, but their shape was simply copied from the mysterious erection, already of fathomless antiquity when the earliest of the Pharaohs spoken of in history took its form as their model.

The great pyramid is not by any means the only monument of Atlantean migrations. We have one in our own country—Stonehenge. For want of the clue afforded by a knowledge of Atlantean history, our antiquarians have blundered absurdly in their speculations as to the origin of Stonehenge. The most absurd guess of all is that put forward by Fergusson, the historian of architecture, who thinks Stonehenge must have been built in the time of King Arthur to celebrate his great battles over the heathen. A somewhat less preposterous theory vaguely assigns its construction to Druids, but the druids, as far as we know anything about them, were not much better than savages themselves, and utterly unable to cope with the problems of engineering involved in the manipulating of the huge stones of which the ancient temple consists.

Atlantean immigrants who came to the country a good deal later than the migration to Egypt — perhaps about 100,000 years ago — were really the engineers of Stonehenge, and they deliberately adopted the stern, rugged simplicity of its design because they were out of patience with the extravagant devotion to luxury and ornamentation then prevailing among the degenerate Atlanteans themselves. At that time Western Europe was all one mass of land extending down from the Scandinavian peninsula to the southern part of Spain. All along this vast coast-line the Atlantean immigrants settled, and put up rough stone monuments, hundreds of which, besides Stonehenge, survive to the present day. A forest of them is to be found at Carnac, in Brittany, and the mysterious remains called "Bolmens," consisting of a few huge stones piled one upon another in the form of rude altars, are all bequests from Atlantis.

But the old stones constitute the least important of the legacies bequeathed to us by the vanished continent. To show how the interest of the Atlantean story reaches its climax, I must explain some mysteries of Nature that have ceased to be mysterious for students of occult science, but still lie within the domain of the "unknowable " by the majority of our contemporaries — the heirs of mediaeval ignorance concerning the origin, growth, and destinies of the human soul. Much that is generally unseen in and around this world is only unseeable by common eyesight. The powers of perception which have already so often referred to as clairvoyance, when developed to a high degree of "perfection, bring into view a vast range of natural phenomena that are absolutely invisible to physical sight, and that is how occultists come to know that which they do know concerning the human soul as an entity considered apart from any particular body which it may animate for a time.

We cannot expect just yet to find the professional clergy leading inquiries of this sort. They are timid about exact knowledge in such matters, as they always have been since the days when they were timid about admitting that the earth was round, or, more recently, in admitting that it can have existed for more than six thousand years. But the best of them are already falling into line with advancing knowledge, and eventually they will all come to see that occult teaching concerning the genesis, growth, and progress of the soul is quite in harmony with all that is essential in the foundations of religious belief. I merely say that, in passing, to guard against a possible misapprehension. The task of showing how religious beliefs, properly understood, are in harmony with real spiritual science would be one I should gladly undertake, but it would, for the moment, constitute too long a digression.

The fact that the soul, as an entity, survives the death of the body, is the one great all-important fact that has been established on a basis of irrefutable certainty by the investigations of the spiritualists. But, in the opinion of most occult students, they have not done much more than establish that fact. People who have passed over may, under some Circumstances, if they wish, communicate with still living friends; but they do not at once know all that is going to happen to them, any more than a baby just born on this plane of life knows all that is awaiting him in life. And, later on, they pass out the conditions which make communication possible — at all events, in the ordinary spiritualistic way. «So the occult student who wants to know a great deal more than his lately deceased friend can tell him, has to fall back on other sources of information. Theosophical books will explain the nature and credibility of these other sources of information. For the moment I can only deal with results. Readers who may be sufficiently interested to want to know in detail how these results are reached, must be referred to the books.

The all-important fact that has been ascertained about the destinies of the soul is that, after prolonged experiences on higher planes of Nature, some of which go far to realise the conventional idea of Heaven, every human soul is born again on earth in the ordinary way, and runs the race of life anew. This supremely important truth is known to occultists as the doctrine of "Reincarnation," and, when properly understood, it illuminates the dark mysteries of earth life as the sunrise illuminates a landscape. It clears away ninetynine hundredths of the painful enigmas of life. The inequalities of health, mental capacity, and worldly station assume an entirely new aspect for the man who realises that each life any one of us is leading is merely one of hundreds through which he has passed in bygone ages; only one in the long series still before him. As in the course of a single life there may be days of enjoyment and days of sorrow or pain, periods of good health and periods of bad, so in the long series of lives which each human being has to go through some will be irksome and troubled, others will be sunshiny and joyous.

In the long account there is a far nearer approach to equality of experience than a glance round at any given moment of the world's history would lead us to suppose possible. Those who may now be doing the rough work of the world are from any true sense victims of the accident of birth: they are (ignoring exceptional cases that can be explained in other ways) the younger members of the human family, subordinate to their seniors for a time. All have been through the same sort of mill in their time, and all have emerged from humbler conditions of existence through which they have passed in remote ages of antiquity, or perhaps much more recently. "But we don't remember former lives," people will be sure to answer. To which I reply: "Most of us do not, but some of us do!" Most of us do not because we have not yet evolved the faculties required for such draughts' upon the universal memory of Nature.

And beyond that, students of occult science can quite clearly see why, at present, it is not provided for in the scheme of things that all should remember. To go into that explanation fully would take too much time, but I may give any thoughtful reader the clue to the puzzle by suggesting that moral responsibility increases with knowledge. More is expected from those to whom more is given, and, as I repeat, there is no such thing as the so-called "accident of birth." The conditions of life to which, at each returnee earth, each soul is consigned, are determined by his own acts in the past life as certainly as the sum total of a column of figures is determined by the magnitude of the items. Of all the mysteries of Nature none are of deeper significance or of greater importance than this sublime system of reincarnation going on around us every minute — for "every minute dies a man, every minute one is born " — and every minute vindicating for those who have eyes to see the justice that rules the ultimate destinies of man.

And now I think it will be obvious that I was entitled to say there are bequests from Atlantis on the stage of this century of greater importance than the old stone ruins that have survived from the Atlantean period. We ourvelves are the bequests of Atlantis! They were not our ancestors, in the common acceptation of the 'word' who lived in the lost continent. We lived there in our time, and worked or played, sinned or suffered, profited by or neglected our opportunities, as the case may have been, and in variegated experience since that long-forgotton era have been reaping the consequences of our action, and either getting credit with the rulers of destiny, or deepening our unfortunate indebtedness. For all of us, as soon as we understand our own nature aright, research into the early history of our race is not a mere exercise of the mind or a gratification of antiquarian curiosity, but a deeply instructive examination of our own life history.

CHAPTER VI. More Atlantis

(This is another article on Atlantis, added in later editions. It complements chapters IV and V.)

"My friends," said a simple-minded preacher once in the hearing of one of my friends, "this world is very old. It is six thousand years old!" Of course, the good man thought he had Scriptural assurance in support of that estimate; but the progress of knowledge has induced us, not to treat Scriptural statements with disrespect, but to read them in a new way, and thus all educated people in the present age are well aware that the planet on which we live has been slowly brought to its present degree of perfection during a great many millions of years, and that the six thousand of our primitive ancestral belief is rather a phase of the present time than a period that can be treated, in any comprehensive sense, as the past.

A fragment of an old Egyptian history, the bulk of which has been lost, gives us a catalogue of kings and dynasties covering a period that has been variously estimated at from 3,500 to 5,000 years before Christ; but everyone admits that remains apparently associated with the earliest part of this period are of a kind that must have been preceded by long ages of civilization.

Professor Flinders Petrie, who has done a great deal of patient work in Egypt, helps himself to another two thousand years. I propose to show the reason we need not submit to those narrow limits in considering the past civilisation of Egypt, and why it is desirable to attack the problem in quite a different way from that adopted by Professor Petrie, if we set out in search of general conclusions concerning the antiquity of civilised mankind on earth, irrespective of any particular area within which such civilisation may, at a given period, have fermented.

Whenever this investigation is seriously undertaken by the scientific world, it must centre round the great problem of Atlantis. I have said that we have no literary records concerning the remote past, but that remark may be qualified. We have none that are as yet universally accepted as trustworthy, but Plato has left us some account, flavoured, it is true with obviously fabulous details, concerning the existence, at a period long anterior to the earliest known dynasties of the Egyptian catalogue, of a great island or continent situated in the middle of what is now the Atlantic Ocean. He got his information from Egyptian priests. Till recently the whole story was treated as a fable, but modern research has gone far, by ordinary methods, to establish the fact that such a continent as he describes did really exist at one time. Of course there is nothing at variance with accepted scientific views in that belief.

Geologists freely admit the broad principle that most of the land which is dry at the present time was once under sea water, and presumably, therefore, that a great deal of the present ocean bed was once dry land. The only reason why the former existence of Atlantis is not universally recognized is that, as yet, we are not supposed to have sufficient proof of its existence. So far, only some students of the subject think the proof, along ordinary lines, sufficient and complete. Some of the scientific men connected with the ocean surveys of the *Challenger* are disposed to regard the configuration of the Atlantic bed as fully establishing the Atlantis theory.

Donnelly, the American writer, brings forward a mass of testimony to show that the ancient beliefs, the artistic work and the natural phenomena - the plants and animals - of Mexico and the Mediterranean basin had a common origin, which could only have been possible if at one time those parts of the world were in touch with each other along land communications, instead of being separated by great expanses of ocean as they are now. And since Donnelly wrote his book, some overwhelming testimony has been forthcoming to confirm the Atlantean story. But before I come to that, it will be convenient to describe how it comes to pass that students of occult science have rushed on enormously in advance of investigation along commonplace channels of research, in reference to the conditions of the world's civilisation at the time when Atlantis was in full life and vigour.

The faculty of clairvoyance, of which I have already spoken in reference to the power it gives to some of its most gifted exponents of examining the structure of atoms far too small for any microscopic investigation, is equally applicable to the investigation of the world's history in long past ages. A time will most certainly come when this wonderful power will be recognised as the most potent instrument of research which science can employ. As yet it is exercised in perfection by only a few persons known to me, but within the Theosophical connection there are several sufficiently endowed and developed - for the faculty requires not merely a natural gift, but great perseverance and devotion to the task, for its effective culture - to provide for the comparison of observations one with another, to eliminate occasional errors, and to fill up detail when the problem in hand has to do with the investigation of some long past period.

In that way the modern devotees of occult science have at last put together such a mass of information relating to the Atlantean period, that we really know much more about it than, for instance, about the so called historical period of Egyptian civilisation. And we have been made actually acquainted, in connection with this research, with dates at which great changes in the configuration of the earth's geography have taken place.

1. The World as it was 800,000 years ago.

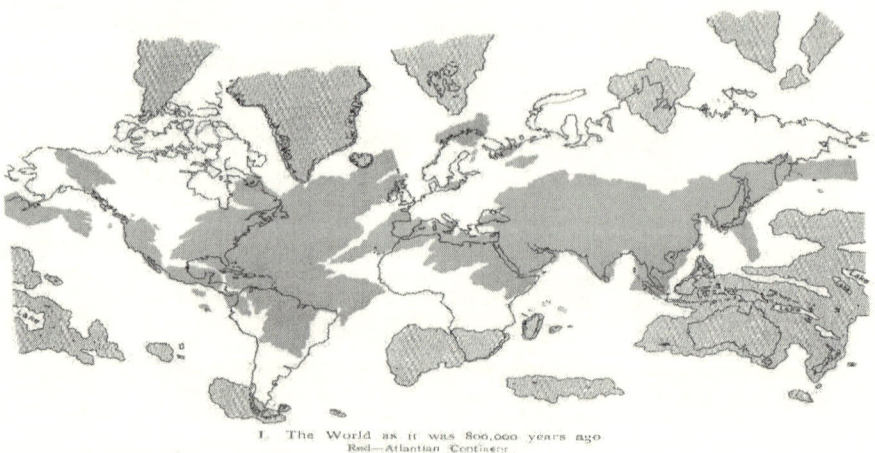

1. The World as it was 800,000 years ago
Red—Atlantian Continent
Grey—Lemurian Continent

Ordinary geology, as I have said, makes it certain that such changes have taken place, but it does not tell us when they happened. Clairvoyant research does tell us when the changes occurred, and more than this, gives us actual maps of the earlier configurations.

"The Story of Atlantis," the results of clairvoyant investigation into that most interesting period of the world's history, has been published in a book bearing that title. ["The Story of Atlantis" by W Scott-Elliot, Theosophical Publishing Society. See also "The Child's Story of Atlantis" issued by the same firm.] The whole narrative is too elaborate and fascinating in its interest to be dealt with in detail in this article, which

has necessarily been concerned with collateral matters, but I want especially to explain how the knowledge we occult students possess concerning Atlantis clears up questions connected with the early history of Egypt that would be quite unmanageable in any other way. Knowing how the geographical changes have been going on, we can reconcile the 9000-year limit (reckoning back from the present time), which Professor Petrie assigns to the whole history of Egypt, with the fact, of which in other ways we are quite equally sure, that the grandest civilisation of Egypt was flourishing many tens of thousands of years before the country entered upon that 9000-year period. That period did not, in real truth, represent its growth and development, but merely its gradual decay.

Once upon a time - I will go into more exact detail later - land stretched almost uninterruptedly right across the region which is now the Atlantic Ocean, from the land we now call Mexico - the extreme westerly limit - to the northern shores of what is now Africa (the southern part of Africa had not then as yet come into existence), and so on right across what is now Egypt (there was no Red Sea then) to what is now Asia. The land, in fact, at the time I am speaking of made a huge belt round the earth. There was no North or South America, no Europe, no South Africa. Much later on, through successive changes that I will not stop now to describe, some approximation to the present condition of affairs was reached, but still there existed in the middle of the Atlantic Ocean an island - the remnant of the original vast continent of Atlantis -and this island was about as big in area as all modern Europe, without Russia. The Red Sea had been invented by that time (it was the result of changes that took place about 80,000 years ago), and so matters remained without any great further alteration until about 11,500 years ago. [The reader should refer to the two maps. No 1 illustrates the conditions first described; No 2 shows the enormous changes which had taken place up to 11,500 years ago.]

That was the period during which the grand civilisation of Egypt was actually in progress. Why have its traces not been more definitely identified? Because at the date last mentioned, 11,500 years ago, the latest of the great cataclysmic convulsions that have from time to time altered the configuration of the earth took place. The vast island constituting the remains of Atlantis subsided with terrific suddenness, and the sea, which then covered what is now the desert of Sahara, was driven eastward so as to completely deluge the land of Egypt. The great pyramid, already in existence (modern archaeology is utterly mistaken as to the date of its construction), was for a time under water. Lower Egypt was obliterated as a region of land, and spent a good many years as so much sea-bed. All traces of the old civilisation disappeared except as regards some of the temples, which, like the great pyramid, are really prediluvian, and when the next change took place, which elevated, to some extent, the whole of Northern Africa and shouldered off the waters of the Sahara Sea, leaving that region to dry up and become a desert, then the Nile resumed business as a river channel, and set to work to make a new Egypt by the deposition of fresh mud. It is this, its latter-day task, that the modern archeologist treats as though it had occupied the whole past time.

The World as it was 11,500 years ago

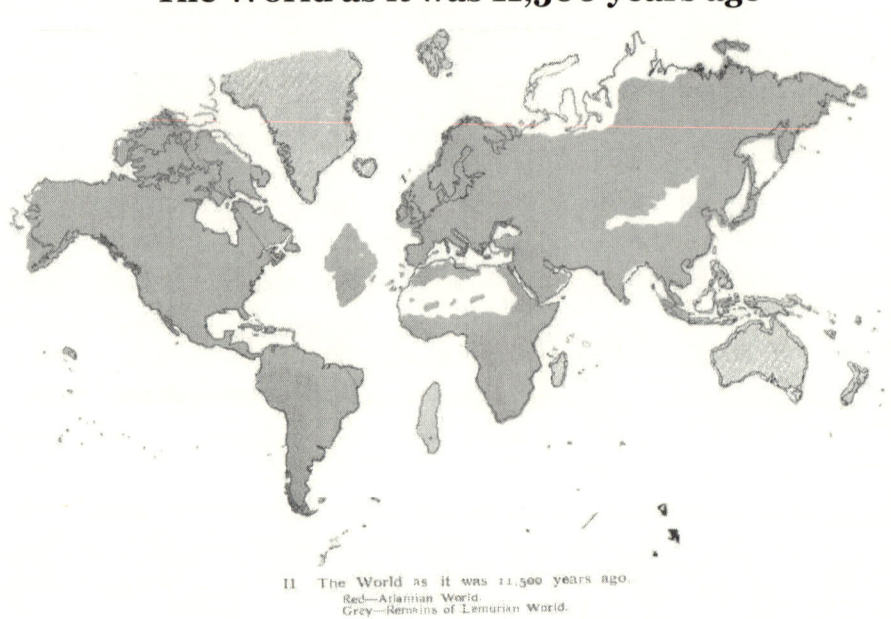

11 The World as it was 11,500 years ago.
Red—Atlantian World.
Grey—Remains of Lemurian World.

And now, having stated what *did* occur -as occult students ascertain by surer methods than the guesses of archaeology -let me, in conclusion for the present, show how some commonplace testimony of the ordinary kind has lately cropped up to vindicate occult research in reference to the latest period of Atlantean history and the final disappearance of the last remaining island. Mexico, as I have said, has from immense antiquity been habitable land. A French archeologist, Dr Le Plongeon, has been at work there for many years. He has written books about his discoveries, and he has been the first person to decipher the Mexican hieroglyphics (which differ from those of Egypt). In 1803, Mr E J. Howell, in the course of a lecture before the Society of Arts, recounted the contents of letters he had received from Dr Le Plongeon concerning his then recent work. He had succeeded in translating a certain manuscript known to archaeologists as the Troano MS. It had never before been deciphered, but Le Plongeon found it to contain a straightforward narrative of the submergence of Atlantis. It is in itself an ancient Mexican manuscript of immense antiquity, and it says that the catastrophe took place "8060 years before the writing of this book." Ten countries, it says, were torn asunder in the convulsion, and sank with their 64,000,000 inhabitants. The date given, it will be seen, fairly well corresponds with that obtained by clairvoyant research, and it is not creditable to the ordinary non-occult students of the bygone history and past evolution of our race, that Le Plongeon's great discovery should, so far, have excited so little attention.

The real, grand, early civilisation of Egypt was introduced by migrations of enterprising colonists from the great Atlantean continent long before the contraction of that continent to the dimensions of the island which lasted till 11,500 years ago. Everything, in fact, in any part of the ancient world had an Atlantean origin, just as a few thousand years hence everything then existing about the world in the shape of civilisation will necessarily be recognized as having had a European origin. Nobody can begin to understand the old world, or the beginnings of the civilisation in the midst of which we live, until he has obtained a comprehensive grasp of the state of mankind in the Atlantean period. Atlantis is the key to all knowledge concerning the past history and evolutionary progress of our race.

CHAPTER VII. Astronomy Ancient and Modern.

The light that has been shed upon the early civilisations of mankind by the story of Atlantis, with which I have been engaged in the last two chapters, will incline people who appreciate its value to take a relatively modest view of modern scientific achievement. Instead of regarding that as an altogether new and original result of modern enlightenment, it will be seen that we are only now beginning to recover knowledge which was the common property of mankind in ages so remote from all those of which we have any literary records, that we can only now get in touch with them by new methods of research, available, as yet, for only a few abnormally-gifted persons. But, at the same time, a correct understanding of Atlantean science, and a comparison between that and our own, need not leave us in any condition of mental humiliation.

The Atlanteans, it is true, were in possession of some highly important natural knowledge which we have not yet recovered, and they seem to have acquired this by devoting themselves much more ardently than we have done to the study of forces inherent in the nature of the human creature. But the characteristic of modern science has been great accuracy and precision in reference to the purely physical aspects of Nature. Roughly summing up the matter, one may describe Atlantean knowledge as due to the application of the human will to the investigation of unseen mysteries in Nature, while that which has been acquired in the nineteenth century has been due to the perfection of instruments applicable to research. These cannot do more than make us acquainted with the gutsides of things, so to speak, but the accuracy with which they accomplish that result is charming to the mind in a very high degree, and may be laying the foundation of a very much more intelligent comprehension of the inner nature of things, when that, in turn, comes within the range of modern investigation, than was attained to by the Atlanteans — though they could make gold, navigate the air, and slay their enemies by the exertion of will in a manner that we (happily for us, perhaps, as regards the last detail) have not yet rediscovered. We have reason to belief that the Atlanteans did know something about the stars and planets that is not at present included in the consciousness of modern astronomers, but they did not apparently possess any instruments worthy of comparison for a moment with those in familiar use today at every observatory in Europe.

People who do not make a special study of astronomy credit modern astronomers with too much knowledge in one direction and with too little in another. I am going to try and show first what kind of knowledge they do possess in perfection, and then, where and why' their limitations come in. If we wanted to select one word which should be the key-word, as it were, of modern science, a single word to be its motto, that word would be " measurement." It is by accurately measuring distances, magnitudes, temperatures, weights, and so on, that 'the grand results of ' chemistry, physics, electricity, as well as those of astronomy, have been reached. Modern scientists are fanatical about the importance of measurement. A chemical analysis must be quantitative to have any value. The energies of an electric current must be expressed in terms which measure its volume? its intensity, its power of overcoming the resistance of various kinds of conductors, with the minutest conceivable accuracy. In dealing with the characteristics of light, we must use the ten-millionth of an inch as the unit of measurement when we are talking about wave lengths. And in astronomy, instruments are used that will measure distances in the sky that are no greater than would be covered by a human hair held 36 feet from the eye.

We reach, in astronomy, a series of conclusions about the distances from us of some of the fixed stars. These conclusions rest upon observations of apparent movements of such stars against the background of the sky, as they are observed at intervals of six months when the earth has completely crossed over to the other side of its orbit. But though that crossing means that the earth is 180 millions of miles away from its previous position, the apparent movement of the star is not greater than the diameter of a penny looked at from a distance of two miles. None the less are the instruments used of such exquisite mechanical perfection that they can deal quite successfully with these minute measurements, and bring out results which we feel sure are approximately right, though the figures used to express them are beyond the grasp of the imagination.

Measurement has been so fundamental a principle in connection with the work of the modern astronomer, that for a considerable time his knowledge did not extend much beyond celestial measurements. These, of course, had to do with other ideas besides those of distance. The orbits in which the planets moved came under the searching eye of instrumental measurement, and, applying mathematical laws to each set of figures obtained by observation, other figures equally trustworthy could be deduced. Thus we came to know definitely all about the density and mass — practically the weight — of the planets and of the sun. And figures of this kind, though at the first glance they may seem to leave us knowing very little about the heavenly bodies in question, are instructive in themselves by enabling us to realise the scale on which the universe is constructed. The distances we have to talk about in reference to our solar system alone are terribly stupendous. The earth swings round in space at a distance of more than ninety millions of miles from the sun, but we are quite near compared with some of the other planets of our family. Jupiter is five times as far from the sun as we are, and the outermost planet as yet discovered, Neptune, is thirty times as far, or over 2700 millions of miles away. The light by which we see Neptune has to radiate out from the sun to that planet, and then come back to us, and though light travels at the rate of 186,000 miles per second' it takes over four hours on the voyage out and home when it illuminates Neptune for our benefit. These figures give one some sort of idea concerning the magnitude of the solar system as a whole. And yet the orbit of Neptune, which may be thought of, for the present, as including the whole solar system, bears a surprising relation to the region in space that is, so to speak, allotted to the solar system.

If you imagine that region a spherical space extending to the nearest of the fixed stars, how big would that space be compared to the diameter of the system itself, the orbit of Neptune? The answer is, that if we had a flat map of that spherical region, and drew it so that the circle was about equal in area to Lincoln's Inn-fields, then the whole solar system would have to be represented by a shilling in the middle. Thousands of millions of miles are as nothing compared with the distances of the fixed stars. The nearest of them is twenty or thirty billions of miles away from us, and a billion is a million million. These figures are almost meaningless to mind, but they have been twisted into all manner of shapes by various writers on' astronomy in the hope of rendering them a little more suggestive. If there was a railway to the nearest of the fixed stars, and the fare for passengers was a penny for a hundred miles, what would be the price of the through ticket? The answer is a sum about equivalent to the National Debt of England. How long would the journey take you, travelling at the ordinary rate of a good express train, or, say, sixty miles an hour? The answer is too big to be helpful to the mind. It is over 50 million years. Light, the speed of which I mentioned just now, takes three years and a half to come from the nearest fixed star, and the distance of the brightest star in the heavens, Sirius, is such that light takes twenty-two years to reach us from that wonderful orb.

Facts of this kind can be observed out to us by modern astronomers to any extent we desire. And besides the measurements they are enabled to undertake, astronomers can now reach conclusions that are more interesting even than their figures. Other sciences have lent their arm to astronomy, and, above all, that which enables us to discover, from the examination of light, the chemical constitution of the body which emits it. The light to the eye may look just the same whether it comes from highly-heated carbon or from highly-heated iron. But to the spectroscope these two kinds of light look very different indeed. The trained observer can recognise one from the other at a glance. And so every kind of substance known to chemistry, when 'heated sufficiently to be luminous, gives out its own kind of light, and no other. In this previously unexpected way astronomers were suddenly put in possession of a resource, an instrument, by means of which they were enabled to ascertain first what the (pun was made of, and eventually what each star that shines with its own light is made of.

This method does not tell us what the planets of our own system are made of, because they merely reflect the light of the sun. They do not give out any of their own- But as far as the solar system goes, spectroscopic research shows us that the sun, anyhow, is made of practically the same elements as the earth; and as independent reasoning along another line seems to show clearly that all the bodies of the solar system were born, in the first instance, from one great nebula, or cloud, of intensely-heated matter — so hot as to be all in the gaseous state- it is reasonable to infer that all the planets are made of the same materials, though it is not necessary to suppose that in each of them those materials would be found in the same proportions. "Elements that are rare with us may be in great abundance in Mars or Venus, and vice versa. There are some interesting ideas hanging on to that suggestion, ""but they belong to the region of speculative astronomy, and, for the moment, I am concerned with giving a general view of the kind of knowledge that modern astronomy really has attained to another kind of knowledge coming within the reach of astronomy when the spectroscope was invented, was that which revealed the true character of the faint cloudy patches of light discernible all about the heavens with the aid of good telescopes, though none of them are visible to the naked eye. These " nebulae " were thought at one time to be no more than masses, or clusters, of very distant stars, so far off that no telescope would " resolve them, as the phrase is, into separate points of light. Now we know that solid bodies give out one kind of light, and highly-heated gaseous bodies another kind, so it is demonstrable which of the nebulae are star clusters not resolved, and which are true nebulae — masses of glowing gas in the state our system was in once upon a time, at a periods remote in the past that the beginnings of the Atlantean age would be is yesterday in comparison. Those true nebulae may therefore be safely regarded as solar systems in course of formation, destined to be the home of life and evolution at some period in the future so inconceivably distant that way, that the contemplation of such a range of time is almost more bewildering — because one shade nearer the possibility of realisation — than the hopeless enigma of eternity.

So, creeping on from one step to another, modern astronomy has come to include a great volume of knowledge concerning what I have called the outsides of the heavenly bodies. I have not by any means completed the catalogue of its achievements in that direction. It has learned a great deal about double and multiple stars; something about comets; it has engaged in plausible and reasonable guesses concerning the origin of stars that suddenly blaze up into intense luminosity, and then rapidly decline again in lustre. To some of these interesting departments of modern astronomy I must return on some other occasion; but, for the moment, what I am wanting to suggest is this: A great deal more may, perhaps, be ultimately learned about heavenly bodies, or, at any rate, about some of them, than is concerned merely with their outsides. Occult science here comes in, and has, at all events, something to tell us about some' of the heavenly bodies that no telescope, no spectroscope, no mathematical calculations can reveal or even hint at.

The methods of research applied to the elucidation of the Atlantean problem are applicable, to some extent, to the investigation of other worlds besides this. Certainly, when clairvoyant research is pushed beyond the limits of our own world, it can only be employed to deal with broader questions than those it may be employed to solve in reference to the history, however remote, of our own race. But still it can tell as much that is of absorbing interest in reference to the other planets of our own system, and in reference to the early development of this system from the incandescent material out of which it was built. And, independently of such information, there are mysteries connected with the relationship, so to speak, of the various planets, and even of the distant stars, with one another which are not suspected by commonplace astronomy, and which, indeed, lie hopelessly and for ever beyond the reach of the methods of research that astronomy has employed so creditably and to such great advantage. Let no one imagine that the true occultist despises the achievements of their painstaking, beautifully precise, and accurate physical science that has been the glory of the century just complete. But there are other ranges of natural research to be respected also by those who know what they are talking about, and in the next chapter i shall have something to say about the occult side of astronomy.

CHAPTER VIII Astronomy Ancient and Modern II

(Another article on astronomy added in later editions)

People who do not make a special study of astronomy credit modern astronomers with too much knowledge in one direction and with too little in another. I am going to try and show first what kind of knowledge they do possess in perfection, and then, where and why their limitations come in. If we wanted to select one word which should be the key-word, as it were, of modern science, a single word to be its motto, that word would be "measurement." It is by accurately measuring distances, magnitudes, temperatures, weights, and so on, that the grand results of chemistry, physics, electricity, as well as those of astronomy, have been reached. Modern scientists are fanatical about the importance of measurement. A chemical analysis must be quantitative to have any value. The energies of an electric current must be expressed in terms which measure its volume, its intensity, its power of overcoming the resistance of various kinds of conductors, with the minutest conceivable accuracy. In dealing with the characteristics of light, we must use the ten-millionth of an inch as the unit of measurement when we are talking about wave lengths. And in astronomy, instruments are used that will measure distances in the sky that are no greater than would be covered by a human hair held 36 feet from the eye.

We reach, in astronomy, a series of conclusions about the distances from us of some of the fixed stars. These conclusions rest upon observations of apparent movements of such stars against the background of the sky, as they are observed at intervals of six months when the earth has completely crossed over to the other side of its orbit. But though that crossing means that the earth is 180 millions of miles away from its previous position, the apparent movement of the star is not greater than the diameter of a penny looked at from a distance of two miles. None the less are the instruments used of such exquisite mechanical perfection that they can deal quite successfully with these minute measurements, and bring out results which we feel sure are approximately right, though the figures used to express them are beyond the grasp of the imagination.

The distances we have to talk about in reference to our solar system alone are terribly stupendous. The earth swings round in space at a distance of more than ninety millions of miles from the sun, but we are quite near compared with some of the other planets of our family. Jupiter is five times as far from the sun as we are, and the outermost planet as yet discovered, Neptune, is thirty times as far, or over 2,700 millions of miles away. The light by which we see Neptune has to radiate out from the sun to that planet, and then come back to us, and though light travels at the rate of 186,000 miles per *second*, it takes over four hours on the voyage out and home when it illuminates Neptune for our benefit. These figures give one some sort of idea concerning the magnitude of the solar system as a whole. And yet the orbit of Neptune, which may be thought of, for the present, as including the whole solar system, bears a surprising relation to the region in space that is, so to speak, allotted to the solar system.

If you imagine that region a spherical space extending to the nearest of the fixed stars, how big would that space be compared to the diameter of the system itself, the orbit of Neptune? The answer is, that if we had a flat map of that spherical region, and drew it so that the circle was about equal in area to Lincoln's Inn-fields, then the whole solar system would have to be represented by a shilling in the middle. Thousands of millions of miles are as nothing compared with the distances of the fixed stars. The nearest of them is twenty or thirty *billions* of miles away from us, and a billion is a million million.

Facts of this kind can be served out to us by modern astronomers to any extent we desire. And besides the measurements they are enabled to undertake, astronomers can now reach conclusions that are more interesting even than their figures. Other sciences have lent their aid to astronomy, and, above all, that which enables us to discover, from the examination of light, the chemical constitution of the body which emits it. The light to the eye may look just the same whether it comes from highly-heated carbon or from highly-heated iron. But to the spectroscope these two kinds of light look different indeed. The trained observer can recognise one from the other at a glance. And so every kind of substance known to chemistry, when heated sufficiently to be luminous, gives out its own kind of light, and no other. In this previously unexpected way astronomers were suddenly put in possession of a resource, an instrument, by means of which they were enabled to ascertain first what the sun was made of, and eventually what each star that shines with its own light is made of.

So, creeping on from one step to another, modern astronomy has come to include a great volume of knowledge concerning what I have called the outsides of the heavenly bodies. But the temper of mind in which scientific men of the nineteenth century have, for the most part, regarded Nature, has led them to neglect all those aspects of astronomy which do not come within the range of measurement. And the prevailing mental fault of the nineteenth century has been conceit with itself and its own achievements, giving rise to contempt for everything that it did not understand. Traditions handed down from earlier periods of the world's civilisation have been thrown aside as superstition if they did not fit in with knowledge the nineteenth century had acquired for itself. Our tendency to do this has been aggravated by the objectionable shape in which, for the most part, such traditions have come down to modern times. But none the less has this hasty, careless policy betrayed the modern scientific world into taking up an attitude in reference to a multitude of Nature's most interesting mysteries, for which we shall be laughed at by the scientists of the future much more contemptuously even than we have been laughing at the folly of our ancestors.

The study of the heavens in past ages bore fruit of a wholly different kind from that which has rewarded the observations of telescopic astronomers. The prevailing belief was that the stars and planets, the sun and the moon, exercise some mysterious influence on human affairs, and, generally, on the world in which we live. The further back we go in clairvoyant investigation, the more persistent and minute we find this belief to have been, and it survived up to a very recent period. It survives, for that matter, with some modifications, amongst those who know, up to the present time, and will revive with great effect at some period in the future, when, perhaps, the mysteries concerned will be better understood than in the past. But the point I want to make first, before going into speculations concerning the future, is that ancient astronomy -or "astrology," as it used to be called -represented an enormous volume of conviction amongst millions of people far advanced in other branches of knowledge and culture, to an extent that ought to make modern thinkers pause before scoffing at their beliefs.

Our principal difficulty in handling the subject is that we have no authentic record of the theories that prevailed among ancient astrologers in reference to the influence of the stars on human affairs. We only know that they gave an amount of attention to the whole subject, which makes it certain that experience had shown them to be on the right track. They probably had no theory to account for the facts they observed, but they had not fallen into the peculiar vice of our age -that of denying that a fact is a fact if we cannot understand it.

The supremely great mind of Francis Bacon found room for a belief in astrology. Kepler, one of the founders of modern astronomy, avows that a study of the facts has "instructed and compelled my unwilling belief" in the inexplicable relationship of planetary aspects and conjunctions with human affairs; and Flamstead, the first Astronomer-Royal of Greenwich Observatory, was not only a believer in astrology, but a practical astrologer himself, and he cast an astrological figure to determine the probable future of the Observatory itself. Nor has the study been altogether neglected even in our own time. Plenty of text-books are in print, and new ones are often appearing, which teach inquirers the rules of the astrological art as far as it is understood now; and other books on the subject have accumulated great masses of evidence to show that though we cannot see the sense of it, astrological forecasts of the future do continually turn out right. My limits will not allow me to tell stories in detail. I know of one case in which a man's death, by an unusual kind of accident, at something over sixty, was foretold at his birth by an astrologer (long since deceased), together with the leading events of his lifetime.

The books record such cases to an extent that makes the theory of accidental coincidence altogether ridiculous. And in a manner that is profoundly mysterious, but almost invariable, the "horoscope," or map of the heavens, at the time of anybody's birth, will be found to correspond, in certain ways, with his physical appearance. I am not going to guess why certain configurations of the planets and stars at the moment of birth should correspond with the physical characteristics of the child. The idea is so difficult to understand that it looks absurd, and all one can say is that it *is* so, and every student who has the sense to examine the facts before coming to conclusions about them, will bear testimony that it is so.

Unfortunately we have lost touch with the finer details of the astrological art as practised by the scientists of the ancient world, and, so far, the scientists of our world have not taken the trouble to work up the lost knowledge afresh. All that we know of astrology practically in the present day is derived from the writings of the Egyptian philosopher, Ptolemy. The situation is all the more tantalizing because, if we go back far enough, we find that in old Chaldea -the country lying along the valley of the Euphrates -the learned men of the time not only made great use of astrology, but possessed so complete a comprehension of the solar system, that they had anticipated our exact knowledge of the distances and masses of the planets. They seem to have been astronomers, in our sense, as well as astrologers, though in those days measurements were apparently held to be of little importance beside what may be called the human interest of the heavens.

In speaking of Chaldean knowledge, I am, of course, drawing upon the results of the clairvoyant investigation for my facts. This investigation has not yet recovered touch with Chaldean methods of astrological calculation, but it shows that, at a period about twenty thousand years ago, the Chaldean priests constructed their temples on astronomical principles. A series of temples in that country constituted a kind of orrery, or model of the solar system. The great temple in the middle stood for the sun. At distances that corresponded in their proportions with the real distances, other temples represented the various planets, and the sizes were all to scale, though, as we find necessary in drawing a map of the solar system, the Chaldeans had to adopt one scale for sizes and another for distances. Anyhow, the arrangement of the temples showed that they already, at that remote date, knew about the existence of Uranus and Neptune, and apparently they were acquainted with one planet that has long been suspected to exist, but has never yet been seen by modern eyes -the interior little world, provisionally called Vulcan, revolving so close to the sun that it is inside the orbit of Mercury.

Already a fairly widespread appreciation of the situation, as I have described it, is leading a good many people to pay attention to astrology, and some of them get too enthusiastic, fancying that the "science," as they regard it, can tell us a great deal more than is really possible. It is not a science at all in its present condition, but a confused mass of rules imperfectly understood, by which calculations can be made, but for no one of which have we any foundation in reason. All we know is that calculations made along those lines come out right in a proportion of cases that makes all talk of coincidence absurd. But the art -regarding it in that light rather than as a science -is fraught with embarrassments. In its first board application it has to do with "nativities," with figures, or maps, representing the positions of the stars and planets in the heavens at the moment of a child's birth but, first of all, how often is the real, exact moment of a child's birth accurately recorded? An error of five minutes will alter the significance of the figure. And what *is* the exact moment of birth? It is needless for me here to go into physiological details on that point. Enough to say that the child's first cry is the orthodox moment in question, according to most modern astrologers.

Given any moment, it is very easy to "put up the figure," as the phrase goes. All the necessary almanacs and tables are regularly published, and anyone can learn the rules for "casting the horoscope." But to read its meaning is quite another business. For that, an astrologer has to be saturated with a knowledge of all the significance attributed by Ptolemy to the various -almost infinitely various -conjunctions, aspects, relative angular distances, and so forth, of the heavenly bodies concerned. And in order to predict future events, according to the rule-of-thumb methods handed down to us, intricate calculations have to be made as to the places that will be occupied by the planets at future periods. Finally, in regard to nativities, no modern astrologer of intelligence would claim to be able to do more than forecast probabilities. The calculations, as we have to make them now, are either too slovenly to be trustworthy, or too intricate to be accomplished by anybody with exactitude. But there is another branch of astrology called "horary astrology," which does not aim at doing so much as that kind which deals with nativities, but is more easily worked. For choice, it seems more absurd -more hopelessly opposed to reason -than the kind I have been describing.

But experience again floors incredulity. If some really important, momentous question concerning your life, health, fortunes, or happiness is preying on your mind, and it suddenly occurs to you, Could astrology answer this question for me? -ridiculous and preposterous though it may seem, astrology most likely could! You yourself, if you are an astrologer, or somebody else for you -the rules to be followed being a little different in the two cases -must put up a figure, draw a map of the heavens, for the moment at which the idea of doing the thing occurred to you. If you have accurately observed that moment, the work can be done at any convenient time afterwards. Then the map is read according to certain rules (which do not involve any intricate calculations), and the answer stares you in the face!

Perhaps, indeed, the figure will not, so to speak, make sense. It will not be coherent. It will, perhaps, resemble a mass of letters jumbled together at random, as compared with intelligible words. But if it does make sense, it will very generally turn out to tell the truth. That is the wonderful part of the story. You cannot begin to explain why. The whole business is utterly unintelligible, but the facts of experience are stubborn things. When they come within our own experience, we all submit to their force, but when they are gathered up by other people, then there are two ways of looking at them. We may say: That sounds all nonsense, so the people who relate their experience must be telling lies. Or we may say: Our knowledge concerning the mysteries of Nature is, so far, the merest smattering. For anything which really happens there must be an explanation to be got at sooner or later. Since the unintelligible experience is there to guide us, let us examine, investigate, try new experiments, gather together such a volume of facts that the actuality of the occurrence shall be beyond dispute, and then let us set out in all directions to hunt for the clue to the infinite marvel with which we have to deal. For, remember that there is no problem with which scientific investigation could concern itself that is of deeper significance to the human race than this which lies at the root of the astrological mystery. To what extent is the future mapped out beforehand by powers above us? How is this globe on which we live concatenated in its destinies with the other globes wandering in space? What, in the name of all that is bewildering, can be the nature of the unseen influences pouring down on this earth across the awful distances that separate us from the planets and the stars? And how, as they intermingle, do they qualify, modify, or accentuate each other?

The leaders of orthodox thought in the present age of the world, and by that phrase I mean, of course, the leading scientists of the time -for no flattery could now assign that title to the theologians -represent a woeful mixture of good qualities and bad. They are so careful, so accurate, so beautifully painstaking within the limits of their activity, that from one point of view they command enthusiastic admiration. And yet they have so ,many characteristics in common with the Man of Muck Rake in *The Pilgrim's Progress*. They will not interest themselves in anything except the physical plane of Nature. A problem must come within the range of laboratory experiment to *be* a problem for modern science. That is a glorious foundation most assuredly, but it is only a foundation, and the time cannot now be far off when the architects of science will begin to dream of the mighty structure that must ultimately rest upon it, and set themselves to work to gather the new kind of material with which alone that structure can be raised.

CHAPTER IX Foretelling the Future

When people blunder by accident, so to speak, into the paths of occult research, and first become aware, in their own experience, that things may happen which their previous training made them think impossible, it often seems to upset the balance of their judgment. The boundary between the possible and that which they have always been accustomed to regard as the impossible, has been broken down. They do not know where to set it up again. So it arises that I often see half-joking, half-credulous conjectures as to wonders that may be perhaps brought about, or as to stories told of something wonderful that is said to have occurred, which no experienced occultist would treat seriously for a moment. In reality, the regions of Nature in which super-physical events take place are just as much under the reign of law as those which have to do with chemistry or electricity. As I grant that these regions are imperfectly explored at present, it may be that they hold many surprises in store for even the most advanced students. But that may be said of any science. Chemistry itself may have surprises in store for us, but, nevertheless, if we are told that some chemist has accomplished some new result, we know, from previous experience, whether such a result lies within the domain of regions not yet fully explored, or whether it is in flagrant contradiction with existing knowledge. So with tales of occult achievement, I could illustrate what I mean in a dozen different ways, but to begin with, I will deal with theories that are reasonable, and theories which are absurd, in connection with a matter which interests everybody and hinges on to what I was writing about in the last chapter -the problem of foretelling the future.

Palmistry and astrology are only two of the methods that from time to time in the history of the world have been employed with this end in view. Most of my readers will be surprised at the length of the list if I give them a mere imperfect glance at some of the systems adopted in the ancient and mediaeval world for getting forecasts of future events. We may read about geomancy, capnomancy, coscinomancy, bibliomancy, belomancy, hydromancy, pyromancy, rabdomancy, and many others, not to speak of our more recent cartomancy and cheiromancy. These were all systems of divination which the prigs of the nineteenth century classed together as so much fraud and imposture, in total disregard of facts as well authenticated in many cases as any of history or geography. The more intelligent view is that, if events are well authenticated as having occurred, and if they seem at variance with some law we think we understand, there must be some hidden factor in the body of circumstances concerned which altered their significance. I will take an example from the testimony of the first Lord Bulwer Lytton, who, as everybody who knows anything at all about the history of modern occultism will be aware, was a very earnest student of Nature's mysteries.

The system of divination which Lord Lytton chiefly made use of was the first on the above list, Geomancy. It would take too long to describe the practical rules of the art, which, as the name implies, has some supposed connection with movements of the earth, but the "figure" set up to solve any question presented to a geomancist (never mind for a moment the rules by which he sets it up) consists simply of dots or marks irregularly grouped on paper. He reads the significance of these markings according to other rules. In 1860 Lord Lytton put up such a figure to see what would be the future of "Mr Disraeli," as he was then -and, remember, the period was one at which it was still the fashion among Liberals, then predominant in Parliament, to ridicule and despise Disraeli -and long before he had ever been Prime Minister. Lord Lytton was astonished at the significance of the figure. He recorded it as quite out of keeping with any reasonable expectations. It betokened important advantages from marriage, a peaceful hearth, public honours far beyond anticipation, death ultimately in an exceptionally high position, in the midst of general affection and regret. The subject of the inquiry would bequeath a reputation "quite out of proportion to the opinion now (in 1860) entertained of his intellect even by those who think most highly of it. His enemies, though active, will not be persevering; his official friends, though not ardent, will yet minister to his success." The details of this prophecy will be found in the second volume of the second Lord Lytton's life of his father. What is the meaning of such cases, which could be multiplied almost indefinitely? I will give some others from my own experience a little further on, but first I want to suggest some general ideas on all such subjects.

To call such a triumph of divination as that just quoted "coincidence" is the common refuge of stupidity. But it is hopelessly unsatisfactory to attribute a correct divination to the arbitrary markings on paper, which seem all there is to go by. The missing factor in the whole transaction is to be found in the all but invariable circumstance that the successful diviners, whatever method they become attached to, are "psychics" in a greater or less degree -people who have to some extent, however unconsciously, developed the faculty of clairvoyance, the faculty of taking in perceptions by means of a certain sensibility which we may, for convenience, call a sense not yet generally developed. The external rules of the system employed would be of very little use in the hands of a person who was not in any measure a psychic, and in the hands of a person really so endowed almost any mode of divination will sometimes prove successful. The use of the favourite method, whatever that may be, has the effect of concentrating the attention, of stirring up the activity of the sense in question, so that the tangible things observed become, as it were, fraught with a meaning.

This explains the nasty old habit of the Roman augurs, who got into the habit of inspecting the entrails of birds or animals. Modern wiseacres laugh at the idea that such indications of the future could be found in such casual and dirty combinations. They fail to realize how stupid it is to suppose mankind for a long period going on believing in predictions that never come true. Of course, they sometimes came true -the predictions of the old oracles and diviners -because, however dirty and meaningless in themselves were the method of divination employed, the more or less effective clairvoyance of the augurs or diviners put them in touch with the foresight which is possible for people whose consciousness can reach that region of Nature which occultists call "the Astral Plane." I have known really accomplished clairvoyants who thoroughly understood all that I am saying now, and a great deal more, who, nevertheless, would cling to some favourite trick, quite meaningless in itself, as a way of starting the activity of the astral senses. Looking in a crystal ball is one such method. The ordinary man might look for a month and see nothing, but I know several persons (quite unknown to fame, and not "professional") who never look in a crystal for a minute without beginning to see visions of one sort or other. One most genuine clairvoyant of my acquaintance had a trick of gazing intently at the bits of tea leaf at the bottom of a cup as a means of stimulating the astral sense. Arabs of old who watched the flight of arrows (Belomancy), and the modern water-finders who use a hazel twig, and seem to feel it turn in their hands when they come over a hidden spring, are in the same way stimulating clairvoyance.

The human goose who thinks they must be "humbugging" because he cannot see the connection between a hazel twig and an underground spring, is doubly stupid. First, there is no contradiction to any really known law in the theory that there *may* be some such connection (though I do not say there is), but, secondly, the fact that water finders do succeed in locating hidden springs is perfectly well authenticated, while the idea that this can be done by persons gifted with the necessary amount of clairvoyance is no more unreasonable than to suppose that a person with a sufficiently good ear can play a tune he has heard on the piano.

The painful embarrassment we have to face in dealing with this matter arises from the apparent necessity of admitting -if we admit that the future can be foretold -the horrible idea that we are under the dominion of some terrible fate that makes every misfortune or sorrow that befalls us inevitable! To believe that the future can ever be foretold seems equivalent to saying that all future events must be determined by some appalling destiny beforehand; that if we do foolish things, we commit crimes even, those acts were inevitable! We seem drifted in this way into the worst horrors of Mohammedan fatalism. No such grievous conclusions need be drawn from the fullest possible recognition of that which to me, and to all who have made the matter a study, is a certain fact, that very often future events are foreseen; that not infrequently prophetic dreams "come true," and that often the crystal, or even the tea-cup, in competent hands will give warning of trouble, or sometimes promise joys that in progress of time actually come to pass.

The apparent contradiction is explained in this way. In that state of consciousness which we call in occult terminology "being on the Astral Plane," or "reading in the Astral Light," the inevitable result of any body of causes then in operation -that is to say, the effect they would have if nothing happens to disturb them can be perceived in a way impossible down here. A humble analogy may be derived from the position of the man on a ladder looking over a maze in which holiday-makers are wandering about and trying to find their way. In the midst of the twists and obstacles they cannot tell at any given moment whether they are pursuing a path that will enable them to get out, or running up a cul-de-sac. But the man on the ladder can see quite plainly. He can see the obstacle or clear path, as the case may be, which is veiled from their sight; therefore he can foretell whether they will go on or very soon be turned back. In the same way, though the complication of the process is greater, the clairvoyant, seeking to follow out the progress of events, sees what must happen, if things are left to themselves, from the operation of the body of causes in existence at any given moment.

But here we are not in presence of an unalterable set of facts like the obstacles in a maze, but are dealing with alterable conditions affected by the human will. Most generally it will happen that, by reason of their blindness to the tendency of subtle causes affecting human affairs, people do nothing to alter the course of events in such cases as I am imagining, and then the prophetic vision, the forecast of the clairvoyant, or the dream, as it may sometimes be, is justified by the event, and "comes true," as the phrase goes. Where the person concerned is himself sufficiently alive to the true meaning of a prophecy as to avail himself of the warning it may convey, he very likely *does* do something to import a new factor into the transaction, and then the event does not come off. That does not invalidate the accuracy of the prophecy. It merely puts the person concerned to that extent in the position of one who has soared above the commonplace conditions of life, and has become, in a certain small degree, a power in the world, not merely a straw borne on the waves of circumstance.

The life of a very remarkable clairvoyant, the late Mrs Anna Kingsford, whose most interesting memoirs have been written by her friend and collaborator, Mr Edward Maitland, will furnish us with examples of both kinds of prevision. In dreams chiefly, but in other ways as well, Mrs Kingsford was continually getting forecasts of future events in which she herself was involved. Many of them would be quite trivial, for it is not the importance of an event that will lead to its prevision, rather the condition of the clairvoyant at the time. In one such case within my own knowledge at the time, as I had the pleasure of her acquaintance, she told friends with whom she was staying just then that she had seen herself in vision, in a hansom cab surrounded by soldiers, and apparently in the midst of some scene of fighting or disorder. No sense could be made of the forecast, but it chanced that the very next day, being in a hansom cab, after calling at a club in Pall Mall to leave a message for one of its members, she was driven rapidly round the corner of Marlborough House and full tilt into the midst of the Guards just marching off the scene of the usual ceremony in the courtyard of St James's Palace. Her unintentional charge threw the column for a moment into disorder. Bayonets were flashing in the sun, the cab horse was on his haunches, and the insignificant scene of the vision was thus realized. Nothing serious happened. The whole transition was of no importance; but she chanced to have sensed the causes leading up to it on the astral plane, and nothing was done to interfere with the results.

In another case, when in Paris, she had caught out a maid-servant in some serious delinquencies. She was very angry, and resolved to prosecute the girl. With this fixed intention in her mind, she slept that night, and dreamed that she saw herself turning the corner of a street in Paris and meeting a woman who threw vitriol in her face. She woke with a sting of the acid, as it were, burning her cheeks. She took the warning, and did *not* prosecute the girl, and the alarming vision never was fulfilled. These are merely two examples out of many that might be quoted from the experiences of the remarkable woman I have named, and from the experience of others less known to fame I could quote other similar cases.

Before dropping the subject, I may as well say a few words on the deplorable manner in which some people sometimes aim at utilizing the possibility that the future may be foretold. There are people who would not hesitate, if they thought it possible, to get occult information as to what horse is going to win the Derby, or what stocks are going to rise or fall. Like every other contingency depending on causes in operation, such events are, in a certain sense, foretellable, because there are few persons concerned with their realization who will be likely to have such knowledge as would enable them to import fresh causes into the combination. But there are two difficulties in the way of degrading the arts of divination to the service of such purposes as those I have indicated. First of all, some of the persons whose apparent free-will is engaged in the business may accidentally swerve from the line of action along which they are being projected by the pressure of circumstances. To discuss that point fully would lead me into the depths of metaphysics, but it is enough to say that such events, as foreseen from the height of astral vision, are liable to disturbance -like all others, indeed. But, secondly -and this is a consideration of greater practical importance -no clairvoyant of the higher order would consent to be engaged in the investigation of such problems. That would involve a degradation of exalted faculties from which every high-minded occultist would shrink, while anyone who might be described as a low-minded occultist would probably not be sufficiently advanced to be guarded against the infinite variety of confusing and erroneous visions with which the astral plane is necessarily saturated.

CHAPTER X. Behind the Scenes of Nature

In a rude and humble sort of fashion the arrangements of a theatre are designed in unconscious imitation of nature's operations in this living world around us. Effects on the stage are presented to the audience, but the machinery by which they are brought about is carefully concealed from view. The visible stage may seem roomy and profound, and the artful devices of the painter may suggest an infinite perspective; but much nearer, really, than the distant hills of the stage picture are the pulleys and ropes that control the shifting scenes. Unsuspected mechanism lurks above and below, and, besides the actors in front of the footlights, many other players of unrecorded parts must be actively at work all the time, or the dawn which has to break over the landscape would not appear at the right moment; the thunder shower, necessary to the progress of the piece, would fail to keep its appointment, and the best sensations of the melodrama might culminate in the shame of the managers. So with the vast proscenium on which the drama of human destiny is worked out; the play could not go on for a day -not for a minute -unless there were countless unseen agencies, many of them quite as intelligent as, or much more so than, those who "strut and fret their hour upon the stage," busily engaged all the time in working the machinery.

A deeper truth than even he intended is involved in the words Lord Bacon used (playing a part himself, and disguised as Shakespeare) when he said, "All the world's a stage, and all the men and women merely players." There are many aspects of the infinite subject I am handling that cannot even be referred to without constant allusion to the unseen agencies so busily at work, and I propose now to give some account of the all-important functions they discharge in Nature, and of the unseen realms in which they carry on their activity. I say "realms" in the plural advisedly, because it would be a fatal mistake to imagine that all "behind the scenes of Nature" is merely one region stocked with the whole mass of machinery which produces the visible effect. There is really region behind region, stretching up to infinity, for that matter, and fading away into the incomprehensible, into that which for ages to come must be the "Unknowable" for most of us; but the fundamental blunder of primitive thinking in connection with these profound mysteries is that which divides Nature into the plainly visible phenomena of everyday life, and a veiled unfathomable region of causation into which it is supposed the consciousness of embodied humanity can never hope to penetrate.

Occult students have penetrated so far into this region that they, in turn, are liable to fall into the mistake of thinking that the whole machinery of the Cosmos is accessible to their investigation. This is far from being the actual state of the case, but none the less is the knowledge we are in a position to obtain so greatly more abundant than that which lies open to mere physical research, that we are at least able to feel quite at home in realms that are, at all events, well behind the scenes of familiar visible

manifestation, and can account for a great deal that seems at the first glance utterly beyond the range of the human understanding.

For the present I shall merely attempt to speak of the region which lies immediately behind the visible world -just as much belonging to the world as its atmosphere. That region is spoken of in occult language as "the Astral Plane." The term is not a good one, because it seems to suggest some association with the stars, though no such meaning is really involved. The phrase, however has been used for hundreds of years by writers on occult subjects all through the middle ages, and we cannot throw it aside now. Again, the word "plane" is not a very happy one, because it seems to suggest a flat surface, and that idea must be utterly cleaned out of the mind before we can begin to think of the astral plane correctly. If we who study occultism, my readers may ask, do not like our own phrases, why do we use them? The trouble is that the language does not supply words that precisely fit occult emergencies.

How, for instance, shall we call this region of Nature, of which I want now to speak, by any really appropriate name? It is a condition of things that in some aspects suggests the idea of an envelope surrounding the earth, but then it interpenetrates the earth as well as surrounding it, just as (or much more thoroughly than) water penetrates the pores of a wet sponge. It is infused in all matter as a salt dissolved in water exists in association with all its molecules. An accepted dictum of occult science tells us that every particle of physical matter has its "astral counterpart." It is through that astral counterpart that all the natural forces controlling its growth or development, whatever that may be, are exerted.

For the most part, ordinary people have no direct consciousness of the astral plane, but dreams often bring them into some relation with it. Dreams have, indeed, a very mixed constitution. When a body is asleep, the consciousness of the person concerned is really, in most cases, in touch with the astral plane, though, unless he is gifted with 'psychic' attributes, he perceives its phenomena very imperfectly. We all have organisms adapted to consciousness on, or with reference to, *all* the planes of Nature;

but most of us at this stage of human evolution have got no more than an astral body in an undeveloped state, not much better ready to work with than the body of a blind kitten a few days old is ready to catch mice. The race will greatly improve in this respect by degrees, but, so far, the people who can exercise consciousness on the astral plane quite completely are few, and that is how the many (when, besides being backward in evolution, they are conceited enough to think they are in its van) are so comically contemptuous about the knowledge that the (relatively) few possess.

Imagine a country isolated from the rest of the world, in which all the people from time immemorial had been born deaf. Life would have adapted itself to that condition of things. People would communicate by signs, and would have become so skilful at that as to be under no sense of restriction. Then suppose, one by one, a few of them began to hear. The early possessors of the incomprehensible faculty would not have a very good time of it among their friends. If they pretended to be able to communicate with one another through an opaque screen, the sober, common-sense majority would know quite well that they were cheating, though it might be difficult to detect the fraud. If they pretended to "hear" a gun fired at a distance, the one thing certain would be -if it turned out on inquiry, that gun really had been fired -that they had bribed the man who fired it to shoot at a pre-arranged moment. The "hearers" would be unanimously voted liars or victims of hallucination, and they would be apt to give up talking about the new discoveries they had made, until, indeed, they became numerous enough to laugh, in their turn, at the old-fashioned deaf mutes, or perhaps, to do their best to share with the more intelligent of those same deaf mutes the advantages of their acquired sense.

That idea would really parallel the present condition of modern society in regard to the phenomena of the astral plane, and the time has happily come when those who have astral faculties are numerous enough to support one another in amused indifference to the jeers of the ignorant "deaf mutes," and sufficiently impressed with a sense of duty to their contemporaries to describe their discoveries openly for the benefit of all who want to grow. For, in truth, the faculties of astral perception will not grow, as the blind kitten's eyes eventually open, quite of their own accord. The appreciative and aspiring mind must bring certain influences to bear on the process -but that is, indeed, another story -as long as we are still standing on the threshold of the astral plane, realizing for the first time, as we look at the tableau on the stage, that there *is* a wealth of machinery behind the scenes by which it is all brought about.

The first most glaring fact about the astral plane for those who become endowed with the faculty of perception with reference to it, is that there we come into relation again with a large majority of people who have recently died. For them, it is true, it is but an ante-chamber to higher conditions of existence, but it is an ante-chamber in which they will sometime be kept waiting a long time. The astral bodies in which they find themselves functioning will be just the same in substance as those which they possessed, without knowing anything about it, during physical life; and at first, truth to tell, for undeveloped people it is a very imperfect vehicle of consciousness. But for everyone it soon wakes up more or less, and in proportion to the extent that this happens (under the mental and moral influences engendered during life), the enjoyment of the astral period of existence is very significantly affected. But I must not be tempted to go into that matter fully just now, because the main point I have in view is the justification of the broad idea concerning the astral plane, with which I started.

It is the region that may be described as behind the scenes of Nature, not merely because the actors who have just left the stage are to be found there, but because there are other -"people" shall I say? -entities, at all events, who have never been on the stage at all, but are entirely concerned with controlling the machinery, and these are known to occultists as "elemental spirits" or "elementals." They are countless as the sands of the seashore; they vary in efficiency, in degrees of growth, in individuality, as widely as the whole animal kingdom on the physical earth varies. The elementals are the agencies through whose intermediation much of the work of Nature on the physical plane is carried out. In some of their aspects they may be thought of as forces, operative, with scarcely any individual initiative, modifying (rather than giving rise to) the growth of plants and the activities of the inorganic world. In the higher departments of their work they participate in the guidance of even human affairs; and in some cases the human will, developed to the higher degrees of its potentiality, controls them in turn, and so brings about the otherwise unexplainable phenomena concerned with material objects that so perplex the reason at some spiritual *séances*.

Spiritualists generally are apt to attribute such phenomena to the direct agency of their departed friends, but this is a mistake that the more scientific occultist does not fall into. The departed friend, during his sojourn on the astral plane, may acquire knowledge, by means of which he can, within certain limits, induce or control elemental beings to subserve his wishes as regards working wonderful phenomena for the instruction or delectation of his late companions still in the earth life; but, more commonly, startling physical phenomena are produced -through elemental agency -by entities, who, for that matter, may have been at no very remote period in the past in earth life themselves, but have been regularly instructed by higher entities, of whom it would be premature to speak more definitely just yet, to play the part of "spirit guides." The complications of the subject lead me continually to brush the surface of fresh mysteries, which readers who follow these expositions systematically will come to know a good deal more about in time.

We must not think of the elementals, however, as being only concerned with working wonders. They are able to do this because it is their function in Nature to work out the ordinary processes of growth, development, and decay, of meteorological phenomena, of combustion, of earthquake disturbances, of everything that happens in the natural world. Do not let anyone imagine for a moment that these results and processes are due to their volition. The elemental, as a rule, has no volition. He? It? They? -one does not know what pronoun to employ in dealing with such unfamiliar activities -are the means by which, in obedience to sublimely exalted volition, the business of Nature is carried on. Occultism does not dethrone the Deity, be it always remembered; quite the contrary. But suppose some reverent savage were to be content to say, with reference to a locomotive engine, for instance, it is the will of the driver that makes it go! A more intelligent inquirer would want to understand how his will was transmitted to the wheels, and he would find the intermediate "elementals" in the boiler and the fire-box. That is the principle on which the occultist studies Nature, and the boiler is to the engine what the astral plane and its marvellous populations of elementals is to the world in which we live.

CHAPTER XI. "Miraculous" (?) Cures.

I WANT now to turn aside from the main current of thought I have been following hitherto, in order to throw some light on a subject very imperfectly comprehended as a rule, by people who do not make any special study of occultism, but one which can be made, at any rate, partially intelligible without much difficulty. I refer to all those so-called "miraculous" cures of disease reported to take place at Roman Catholic shrines sometimes (and laughed at by ignorant people), alleged also to be brought about by the methods of a certain " sect," if one may so describe them, calling themselves "Christian Scientists," and, furthermore, recorded with vast amplitude of detail in the innumerable books on mesmerism. Here we are in touch with a branch of occult research that has practical interest for everybody. If, to use the public's favourite phrase, there is "anything in it" as regards the actual relief of bodily suffering by simple methods of which, as yet, the doctors as a rule know nothing, then, indeed, people who may not feel drawn to study occultism for its own enchanting sake alone, may see that it is worth while to grapple with such problems seriously.

Mesmerism is the fundamental process to be considered first in connection with the cure of disease by methods which are not those of ordinary medicine, and if anyone in the present age of the world doubts whether mesmeric processes ever have cured disease, he differs only in degree, not in kind, from the natives of equatorial Africa, who doubt whether it is true that water can be made to grow cold enough to turn solid. There is no department of human folly so curiously significant as that which has been concerned during the past century with suppressing, denying, and concealing the wonderful results of curative mesmerism; with persecuting and abusing the few brave men who have stood up in the face of obloquy, and sometimes of private ruin, to proclaim the truth. The modern developments of mesmerism that began at the end of the eighteenth century were mainly concerned with the curative side of the discovery, and the regiments of French books written at the time are almost entirely devoted to records of cures effected, and of the methods to be employed in carrying them out.

But the doctors of the period were furious. They were jealous, alarmed, and angry, and did everything they could to crush and discredit Mesmer and his followers. Poor Mesmer is one of the best misrepresented men of modern history. He was a good, though rather vain and excitable, doctor of Vienna, in the first instance, who accidentally — if there is such a thing as accident in this world — discovered that he could effect cures by means, as he thought, of magnets and influences proceeding from the hand. He associated this influence with the other (groping about rather blindly in the beginning for explanations of what he found to be occurring), and so called the influence "animal magnetism " — an unfortunate phrase which has lingered in use so long that one can hardly now get rid of it, though, really, it is entirely a misnomer. At once he was sneered at and ridiculed for suggesting anything so absurd as that- something with which the wiseacres of 1775 were unacquainted. — so, hoping for a more liberal-minded *clientele*, he moved to Paris a year or two lifter the date just mentioned, and found himself out of the frying-pan into the fire.

Certainly he won over numerous converts to his belief. People, who themselves were cured of otherwise incurable maladies by his means, began to be more impressed by their own experience than by the assurance of their regular doctor friends that such cures were impossible. But the whirlwind of misrepresentation and abuse in which Mesmer lived bore down the evidence of those who benefited at his hands, and he was ultimately hunted out of Paris into poverty and obscurity, and ended his days curing poor people in Switzerland for nothing. Then his followers began to write books (I have shelves-full of them), giving their own - experience and testimony, and the regular doctors fought harder than ever to persuade the world that mesmerism was an imposture, and that, if people were cured by it they were hallucinated, or, if not, so much the worse for the facts."

Dr Elliotson, in this country a physician in good practice, was a dazzling exception. He came to know about the reality of mesmeric cures, and carried them out at a hospital under his control in the north of London. By this time it had been ascertained that mesmerism would sometimes render patients insensible to the pain surgical operations. This was before the days of chloroform, when every operating-room was a torture-chamber. At Dr Elliotson's hospital, the greatest operations were carried out without the patients suffering pain. In one famous case, when a man's leg was cut off in presence of numerous witnesses without any suffering on his part, the achievement was made the subject of a solemn communication to the Medical and Chirurgical Society, and the members of that society were furious. They passed a resolution to the effect that the whole story must be false, because it was contrary to the known laws of Nature, and that even if it were true, it would be flying in the face of Providence, that had ordained pain as a concomitant of surgical operations! I am not romancing. That resolution was actually passed by a body of doctors in the middle of the nineteenth century.

Elliotson was ruined as a physician, and the view of the Medical and Chirurgical Society triumphed for a time. Meanwhile, Dr Esdade, at Calcutta, in charge of the principal hospital there, read about mesmeric cures, and being of opinion that there might be some things in heaven and earth not yet known to the Medical and Chirurgical Society, tried experiments. The results amazed him. He effected extraordinary cures by mesmeric means, and was successful to an equally wonderful extent in making patients insensible to pain during operations. He was so astonished that he took care to get many of the foremost Europeans in Calcutta to come and be present and bear testimony to these wonderful phenomena. His books on the subject give their signed evidence, but all this overwhelming weight of assurance made not a pin's worth of difference to the British doctor. That wonderful person had made up his mind that mesmerism was an imposture, and, therefore, any statement that seemed to imply the contrary must be false.

Then an amusing phase of the great discovery came on. About the middle of the century a Manchester doctor, Braid by name, who had been as fierce as any in denying the truth of mesmerism, accidentally witnessed some of its astonishing "phenomena". He seems to have been in a dilemma. Mesmerism could not be genuine, because in that case he, Dr Braid, and his colleagues would have been proved wrong — an unthinkable absurdity; but it was embarrassing to go on denying possibilities which he knew, and other people knew he knew, to be facts. So he hit upon a clever way out of the difficulty. He imitated some of the simpler phenomena he had seen by methods, we know now, very inferior to those adopted by Mesmer and his followers, and gave the process so degraded a new name. He wrote a book, and said, in effect, "Mesmerism, as we all know, is an imposture, but I have discovered that there is a real force in Nature, which is *Hypnotism,* and that accounts for everything." The difference really between hypnotism and mesmerism is like the difference between a violin and an orchestra. One is a small part of the other, but so ready are people, in general, to go on repeating that A., B., or C. is an impostor if he discovers something far ahead of common knowledge, while D., E., or F. are men of science if they discover something only an inch or two in advance of common knowledge, that, to this day, careless lookers-on continue to think that Mesmer was a humbug, and that Braid is really the father of what is now at last recognised as a fact in Nature, though still very ill-understood for the most part— Hypnotism.

The real difference between the condition brought on by the methods of hypnotism, and that induced by the methods poor old Mesmer practised (without properly understanding them), is this: Hypnotism is a nervous paralysis brought on by certain strains the patient is instructed to apply, either to the nerves of the eye or in some other way. It is not an injurious state to be in. Sometimes it may even have the effect of making the subject insensible to pain, in others it may give the system a rest from which good results ensue as regards particular ailments. But it is a self-induced condition, and the only thing the "hypnotist" does is to tell the patient what to do. Now, the mesmerist produces the same result as regards the possibly beneficial nerve paralysis, but he does something else as well. He gives out to the patient something from himself — that fluid which Mesmer unfortunately called "animal magnetism," and that in some cases may be enormously beneficial to the patient. Of course, if the mesmerist is ailing in any way himself, his "magnetism" (I use the word under protest but one must call things something or other) is distinctly injurious; but if he is a strong, healthy person, it is Life that he is giving to the patient, plus any good effects ensuing from the rest to the system involved in the suspension of activities for a time associated with the hypnotic element in the process.

It would be tedious if I stopped to relate stories of cures effected by mesmeric processes within my own knowledge, I have seen a great deal of such work, and I know that, under favourable conditions, the most formidable ailments, like consumption and cancer, can be cured by mesmerism, not to speak of the many varieties of nervous disorder which some persons — halting half-way towards a proper comprehension of the subject —often fancy to be the only maladies for which it is efficacious. Anyone who likes to take the trouble can read up the literature of the subject, and store his memory with hundreds of well-authenticated cases. Esdaile's book, the many volumes of Elliotson's periodical, The Zoisty; the voluminous writings of Deleuse and Puysegur, or the vast German encyclopaedia of the subject for those familiar with that tongue, will satisfy the most voracious literary appetite. Of my own little book on mesmerism[1] will be found to epitomise the earlier literature. But, for the moment, I can employ the present opportunity better than in repeating ancient history. I can give my readers a clue that may enable them, in some measure, to understand how it comes to pass that influences apparently so insignificant as "passes" — mere movements of one person's hands in front of another —

---

[1] The Rationale of Mesmerism.

can produce great and beneficial changes in the patient's system. Few people brought up in the materialistic belief of the nineteenth century can help laughing at a mesmeric process, if they happen to see it. They think it so ridiculous to suppose that any good can be done that way. They laugh because they have not yet learned that more goes on behind the scenes of Nature than in front of the proscenium. But I must explain some of those unseen activities of which, as yet, I have made no mention, before the true inwardness of the mesmeric pass can be even vaguely comprehended.

What is the difference between living matter — the flesh of animals or the substance of plants — and that which, by comparison, may be called dead matter, the substance of metals and rocks? Of course, the differences are many, but one hugely important difference is this: A certain influence — let us call it a fluid — of a subtle kind, more subtle than the finest gas, pervades the living matter, and is allured in its character by the vital activities of animal bodies, especially by those of the human animal. It pervades the whole world, in reality, and is one of the many unseen radiations that come from the sun in the first instance, but it only becomes what may truly be called vital fluid when it has been absorbed by, and has been characterised in a certain fashion (I must speak vaguely unless I am to write volumes on this subject) by, the laboratory of an animal system. Of course, it is only the healthy animal that can do the work required. The unhealthy one is unable to digest, so to speak, as much of this fluid as he needs for his own continued life. The healthy person can work up a great deal more than he requires for himself, just as the bees make more honey than they really want for themselves.

Now, the first and simplest thing that happens with really good mesmerism is this: The patient is ill or dying for want of the vital fluid in question; the mesmerist has more than he needs for himself, and he bestows it on the patient by means of the passes that the ignoramus laughs at. For, like some of the elemental forces of which I have been speaking, the fluid in question obeys the influence of will, and if it is the intention of the mesmerist that it shall pass from him and benefit his subject, it does so! I have seen people in an enfeebled condition of health revive under the mesmeric influence, just as a half-withered flower will pluck up its petals if put in water. The process is as natural, as free from the element of the miraculous, when properly understood, as pouring milk into a jug.

But I do not say that mesmeric passes will affect everybody equally well. That is the weak point of the system. It is as real as a peal of thunder, but then there are people so deaf that they do not even hear a peal of thunder.

I must go on with this subject a little farther, and try to make it clear why some people are so sensitive to mesmerism that it is for them worth all the drugs in the pharmacopoeia, while others are no more able to feel any effect from it than a brick wall would appreciate the touch of a friendly hand.

CHAPTER XII The Sensitive and the "O.P"

What is the difference between persons who can take up the mesmeric influences and those on whom it has no effect whatever? The fact that this difference exists is one of the reasons why so many people remain incredulous about the reality of the effects that seem to be produced on others. They declare, scornfully, "You can't mesmerise me!" and vaguely feel that, in saying this, they have cast grave doubt on the question whether there is really anything in mesmerism at all. It is as though some person, with no more ear for music than a cabbage, should go away from a concert, declaring, "You can't make me distinguish any difference between *God Save the Queen* and *Pop Goes the Weasel*." If such persons as he were in the majority, then the possession by some of a musical ear would be laughed at and disbelieved just as, in the present state of common knowledge, the condition of "sensitiveness" to mesmeric and other influences of a similarly subtle character is laughed at by the Ordinary Person of today -the "O.P., as we, who to compare him very often with others more highly gifted, have fallen into the way of describing him.

I suppose few people are so little acquainted with the elementary facts of chemistry that they would be surprised to see nitric acid seriously affecting a silver plate, while it produced little or no immediate effect on a plate of lead. The silver is sensitive to nitric acid, and the lead is much less so. With all the science of the Royal Chemical Society to help you, you could not come much nearer an explanation of that state of things than the phrase just used embodies. So, in reference to the more intricate problem why some persons can take up and be seriously affected by an unseen influence like that emanating from the hands of a genuine mesmerist, it would hardly be reasonable to expect that a fully satisfactory explanation could be provided. In truth, we can come rather nearer explaining why some persons are sensitive to psychic impressions -including those on the borderland of the physical and psychic planes - than we can account for the mysterious affinities of the chemical elements; but to content ourselves, in the absence of any perfect explanation, with analogies, I would point to the familiar fact that a sheet of aluminium is almost absolutely transparent to Röntgen rays, while a sheet of platinum is almost absolutely opaque. Both metals, to the eye or touch, seem equally solid and impervious to anything we put upon them. Or again, why should glass be quite transparent to ordinary light, and wood, a more porous substance, quite opaque to it? There need be nothing surprising, though there may not be any conditions quite explicable, in the fact that some human bodies are pervious to the mesmeric fluid, and some impervious to it.

As to whether there is or is not a fluid in the case at all, that can only remain in doubt, with the O.P., by reason of his unfamiliarity with the evidence on the subject. Great numbers of people -far more than those who can bear visual testimony to the reality of astral plane phenomena -can *see* the mesmeric fluid as it streams from the hands of a competent performer, and floats around the subject on whom he is operating. In the middle of the century just past, Baron Reichenbach devoted himself to that particular research, and records experiments with over sixty people whom he found able to see the emanations in question, and a somewhat similar emanation that actually proceeds from physical magnets. People who deny the fluid "theory" of mesmerism might as well deny the north-seeking tendency of the compass needle. There is more evidence for that, certainly, than for the other fact, but there is adequate evidence for both.

How many per cent, of the present generation, it may be asked, are to be regarded as sensitive and how many as O.P.'s? The embarrassment here arises from the wide varieties that are to be observed as regards the degree of sensitiveness of those who are not absolutely impervious to all such influences. In its higher forms of perfection, sensitiveness means a great deal more than the mere susceptibility of being benefited by mesmerism in ill-health. I am coming on to these wonderful conditions later, but keeping just for the moment to the subject of cures, these have to do with the lowest or slightest kinds of sensitiveness. People may be cured of serious diseases by mesmeric methods who would not be capable of going off into a trance, or of becoming insensible to pain under mesmerism. For always remember that sensitiveness is not a weakness, but a faculty. Not to be in any way susceptible of the influence is to have a relatively dull, leaden, or clod-like constitution. Unhappily, that is the condition of most of us at present, but I will show directly how very far it is from being the condition of some.

Before coming to that, however, it may be well to speak of the curious development in certain cases of a peculiar kind of sensitiveness that renders people able to benefit in ill-health by pilgrimages to special places. At first sight there appears to be no connection between ordinary mesmeric sensitiveness and that aptitude for benefiting by the strange influences brought to bear on persons visiting such shrines as those of Lourdes in France, where it is undeniable that cures, thought to be miraculous, have sometimes taken place. In such cases there is no apparent mesmerism to operate. The patient goes to a place where it is popularly believed that some supernatural manifestation has promised a healing influence to those who shall seek it in a devout spirit. In Roman Catholic countries it is generally the Virgin Mary who is supposed to be the author of such promises. Anyhow, people go in full faith, and are in some cases cured of their afflictions, but not in all. What is the meaning of it? The explanation has to be sought partly in the sensitiveness of those who are benefited, and partly in the agencies behind the scenes, which then take the place of the mesmerist.

The problem brings us into relation with the benevolent side of what I have been talking of so much lately -elemental influence. Never mind what may be the real originating force animating the benevolent elementals concerned, the *force* has been actuated somehow, and then the result follows for any persons who are in any degree sensitive. They may think the result due to a direct interposition of Providence. The restoration to health is really as much due to the operation of natural causes as though they had been mesmerised back to health, or had been successfully treated by purely physical means. And, difficult though it may be to follow the train of causation, the same thing, with modifications, has to be said of those cases in which cures are effected by the people who call themselves by the doubly inappropriate name, "Christian Scientists."

It is utterly foolish to ignore the dazzling results these people sometimes obtain, however little their proceedings may seem to fall within any definite category of intelligible mesmeric method. I know of halfa-dozen cases in which serious internal troubles, for which ordinary doctors could describe nothing short of formidable operations, have been decisively cured by the Christian Scientists. Because such people often fail and take money for trying their best, the suspicious O.P., regards them as conscious imposters, to whom criminal penalties ought to be awarded. They seem to be working in the dark, and without any clear understanding of the conditions of sensitiveness, and so they do not know in any given case whether they will succeed or fail. But however tainted all proceedings of this kind become when mixed up with pecuniary interests, the rough and brutal behaviour of the Christian Scientists are apt to encounter in cases of failure, are more discreditable to the intelligence of the period than their own highly unscientific methods are discreditable to them.

But now let us turn from the purely medical aspects of mesmeric practice to those of far greater interest for the student of Nature's mysteries, which link the phenomena of mesmerism with the inquiry into the loftier possibilities of human consciousness. Mesmerism is what one of the early mediaeval writers on occult subjects has called "the Open Door to the closed palace of the King -in other words, the easiest method at our disposal for investigating the natural laws governing the superphysical world. As soon as we find a subject of really fine sensitiveness, we are introduced to psychic phenomena of the most enchanting order. I will begin by describing a few of these that have come within my own experience. The possibility of rendering a mesmeric subject, once put into the state of trance, insensible to pain, leads us on to a very pretty and highly instructive phenomenon. Having put my subject into a trance, and having shown her friends that she was entirely insensible to pain by running a needle into her arm without causing her to move a muscle or an eyelash, I have given the needle to one of her friends and I have said: "Now, at your own discretion, prick *me* anywhere, and you will see *her* give the start." The result has come off precisely in that way.

By-the-bye, having used the pronouns "her" and "she" in the above statement, let me explain that the finer kinds of sensitiveness are more often found in women than in men, not, as the mistaken idea sometimes has it, because the woman is the weaker vessel, more easily dominated by another will, but because women, other things being equal, are the superiors of men in respect to the delicate faculties that are required for sensitiveness. It is a great mistake to suppose that the person who, in the ordinary affairs of life, may be domineering and obstinate, has a "strong will" for mesmeric purposes. He may be as feeble as a child that way, and a meek, submissive woman might have fifty times the mesmeric force. But again, it is not in the mesmerist that the conditions exist that are important in producing striking results. These depend, in a far greater degree, on the characteristics of the subject.

Well, in the absence of occult knowledge, I think it would be safe to defy anyone to give any plausible explanation of the needle experiment I have just described. But it falls into place quite naturally when we have the advantage of considering it in the light of occult knowledge concerning the superphysical principles of the human constitution. The mesmeric fluid, spoken of above as emanating from the mesmerist and floating round the subject, is identical in its nature with the subtle essence that permeates the nervous system, and is, in point of fact, the medium of communication between different parts of the body and the brain. The O.P., physiologist thinks the nerves themselves, that he can dissect out with instruments, are the telegraphic wires that perform this function. So, originally it used to be thought that the copper wire of an ordinary telegraph was the conductor of the electricity; but *Modern Views of Electricity* (Sir Oliver Lodge's book on that subject) holds, rather, that the real channel of communication is the ether surrounding and interpenetrating the copper. I am inclined to think that the right view in regard to physical electric circuits, but assuredly the corresponding view is the right one in regard to the nervous system and the brain. Occult students call the subtle fluid in question (when considered in reference to this function) the "nerve aura."

Now, this nerve aura in a sensitive is very mobile. The mesmeric process drives it out and replaces it with the nerve aura of the mesmerist. The two auras are for a time blended together especially linking the two brain systems. Moreover, by reason of the condition of perfect trance established, the soul of the sensitive has drifted away from the body, and exists outside that body -perhaps close by, perhaps a long way off; but that is another story -in the astral vehicle, or sheath, or body, whatever you like to call it. Now, the alien nerve aura in the subject's system forms a very imperfect medium of communication between her limbs and brain, and this is why she does not feel pain when herself pricked, but there is a very good conductivity in the mass of nerve aura connecting her brain with that of the mesmerist. So, when he feels a prick -in the hand, let us say -his own nervous system conveys news of that occurrence to his brain, and a simultaneous impression is instantly conveyed to hers. Her brain is affected exactly as it would be in ordinary life if her hand were pricked, and so she gives the start, and, as I have seen in such cases, will make an automatic movement of the hand itself.

CHAPTER XIII Photographing the Unseen

Probably almost everybody who may read these lines will have heard, one time or another, of what are called "spirit photographs." These represent, in a more or less shadowy fashion, beings, spirits, ghosts, or astral entities -call them what you like -that are perfectly invisible to ordinary eyesight. The simple reason why such appearances on a photographic plate are not overwhelming in their effect on popular incredulity is that such photographs can be very easily "faked," or fraudulently imitated. Nothing is easier than to dress up a living person in floating drapery, to give a momentary exposure of the plate with this imitation spirit focussed upon it; afterwards to use the same plate for an ordinary sitter, and so obtain the semblance of a ghostly form standing by his side. The value of a spirit photograph depends entirely upon the perfect *bona fides* of the whole operation. And innumerable private photographers, also spiritualists, have taken such photographs themselves, and, knowing that no improper trickery had been concerned with the results, have obtained photographs of spirit faces on their plates.

I suppose there are few professional photographers who, if they told the truth, would not have to confess that sometimes strange effects come out on their plates that seem to represent something "supernatural." But it would not be good, in the present age of the world, for an ordinary photographers's business that he should be supposed to dabble in such "uncanny" achievement, so, when the strange results come out, the ghost is treated as a defect of the plate, and is suppressed accordingly. However, unless the sitters or the photographer, or both, are mediums, such results are unusual. On the other hand, when the photographer is a medium, and lays himself out for the unusual effects, they are exceedingly common. I have seen an immense number of such spirit photographs taken under conditions that have made me quite sure they were genuine, and very recently I have obtained a series under conditions that make any question as to their authenticity altogether absurd for me, and equally so for any other persons who are capable of understanding that I am telling the truth.

I went to a photographer who had been successful in obtaining several such photographs for friends, and, with his cordial concurrence, took precautions which put all possibilities of fraud, on his part, out of the question. I should like to remark that these precautions would have been unnecessary for my own satisfaction, first, because the honesty of the man and his sincere interest in the whole matter make his *bona fides* perfectly obvious to any rational person having to do with him, and, secondly, because I was accompanied by a lady of my own acquaintance, gifted with clairvoyant sight, who could *see* the spirits being photographed. But in order that I might have an answer for people to whom I might be inclined to show the results, and who might not be able to attach importance to the

ideas I have just expressed, I took my own packet of plates - purchased the day before at Whitelay's -went myself into the photographer's dark room, put my initials on the corners of the plates, and arranged them ready for use, saw the first put into the dark slide, and came out with it into the studio, sat, and afterwards saw the plate developed under my own eyes. It bore a spirit form, as did all the others used that morning, more or less completely. [The annexed illustration reproduces this photograph quite correctly, though with less delicacy than the original prints from the negative still in our possession.]

In two cases the faces of the astral entities are as clearly defined as if they had been physical sitters. In some the plates are marked with blurs of light, representing an unsuccessful attempt, on the part of some astral person, to materialise sufficiently for the purpose in view. The failures are as interesting as the successes, almost, for the student of these problems, as they help us to check our theories as to the way the effect is brought about -but of that, more directly. Before going into theory I want to record a few more facts.

A lady of my acquaintance, wishing to obtain spirit photographs, arranged a series of private sittings with a few congenial friends; used her own camera, and, after a few failures, obtained some of the desired effects. But then a very wonderful development ensued. The spirit friends present said (for be it understood that in this case the sitters included some who were clairvoyant and "clair-audient," so that they could converse with the visitors from the astral plane): "Do not bring your camera any more. Merely sit in the dark with a photographic plate in your hand, and we will do the rest." Following these instructions, the lady used to take her plates to the *séance*, unfasten them in the dark, hold them by the corner for a minute, wrap them up again, take them home, and develop them in the ordinary way. Under these circumstances faces used to appear on the plates, together with a quantity of curious and unintelligible markings that covered the rest of each plate; but the faces are in all cases quite distinctly recognisable -in some cases as those of departed friends. I have a collection of prints from these extraordinary negatives by me as I write, and they are a defiance of what ignorant materialistic people call "the known laws of Nature." But, at the same time, they are facts, like Nelson's Column at Charing Cross, and human beings capable of reason have got to revise their views of Nature's laws accordingly.

Now the spirit photographs obtained with a camera like those of my recent series are produced in one way, and the photographs without the camera in another which is less easily explicable; but still I hope to give the reader a clue to the comprehension even of that process. There is really very little that is truly mysterious in the camera spirit photograph. But it has nothing whatever to do with the method by which the unseen in astronomy is photographed. That process is one which should be understood by anyone wanting to understand the spirit photograph, only that it may be put aside as inapplicable. It is interesting enough in itself, and has given us knowledge concerning some phenomena of the heavens that could not have been obtained in any other way.

If you look with the eye of the constellation called the Pleiades, for example, you see a certain number of stars. If you look with a telescope, you see more; but, however many you see in either case, you do not see more by continuing to look. Now, take a photograph of the Pleiades with a short exposure, and the plate will show you much the same effect as the telescope, but the longer you let the camera look at the constellation, the more it will see. That is to say, the very faint light from small stars, or nebulous matter surrounding the stars that are not bright enough to be seen with the eye, produces an effect on the plate by degrees. The effect of the light on the sensitive plate is cumulative, and in this way we have come to know that the whole constellation called the Pleiades is surrounded by a wonderful nebula of colossal magnitude quite too faint to be seen by any telescope.

Again, there is another variety of the unseen that can be photographed on different principles. The peculiar kind of light called the Röntgen ray is not perceptible to the eye, because the vibrations of the ether which constitute that variety of light are too rapid and minute to suite the mechanism of the eye, delicate as that is. Everyone knows that there are sounds too shrill to be heard, and just in the same way -to put the idea paradoxically -there is light too bright to be seen. But the camera can see that sort of light. In other words, the sensitive plate can be impressed by it; hence we get our radiographs of people's bones and all the other phenomena of X-ray photography. And hence also, for the matter is not more complicated than that, do we get our spirit photographs of the ordinary kind -those which are taken with the camera. The spirit may be in a vehicle of consciousness that is not of a kind to impress ordinary vision, and yet it may impress the photographic plate.

How, then, does it happen, an intelligent inquirer may ask, that we do not get superphysical effects on every photograph taken, since we are told that the astral plane is all around us, and the whole of another world always in sight if we could only see it? Just so, but the light emitted from, or reflected by, *astral* matter does not affect the plate. The spirit or astral entity who wants to get himself photographed -and nobody ever yet photographed a spirit who did *not* want to have his portrait taken -has to suffuse his astral body with matter of somewhat different kind, in order that its shape and appearance may become visible to the plate. The matter in question is spoken of by students of occultism as "Etheric," and it exists, though unseen by the eye, in the constitution of every human being. From the constitution of some it is very easily withdrawn by astral spirits who want to borrow it, and susceptibility to that sort of treatment is one of the attributes that go to constitute a medium. Such withdrawal is a weakening, enfeebling process, and that is why mediums often feel very much depleted and exhausted after *séances* at which materialising phenomena have taken place. The materialisation of the spirit sufficiently for the purposes of the photographer need not be carried nearly so far as that which aims at making the spirit actually visible to ordinary eyesight; all the same, it is still more or less of a strain, and spiritualists, generally, who do not study the science of their own experiences, are often foolishly reckless about strains of that sort themselves -indeed, only one kind among many perils that beset the practice of mediumship.

I said the method of X-ray photography was the same as that by which we get the portraits of spirits. That is because of the X-ray is really an emanation, from the "cathode" or negative pole of the electric circuit in a vacuum tube, of etheric matter. Ordinary science has not yet realized this fact, for in many ways it lags behind the knowledge gained by occult research; but such is the fact, and many other interesting possibilities of the future hang on to that fact. To see astral matter, a person in the physical body must have an altogether new sense developed; but to see etheric matter, it is only necessary for the present eyesight to be improved, as already it is improved for some few persons. The eye is an instrument of very varying capacity. This may be illustrated by an interesting experiment with the spectrum.

If we arrange things so that a solar spectrum -the rainbow-coloured band of light -is thrown on a sheet of paper or a screen, it will be found that some people can see colour beyond the violet tint visible to all. That is because the eyes of such persons are enabled to cognise vibrations of a higher order than those which are perceptible to the rest of us. Persons who can see a good deal further in the spectrum than others will probably be able also to see the Röntgen ray. That is to say, such persons have, in a greater or less degree, the etheric sight. When this is perfectly developed, the possessor of such a faculty can see through opaque matter of some kinds -of those kinds which the Röntgen ray penetrates -and are thus endowed with a species of clairvoyance, not of that kind which is the true clairvoyance of astral sight, but of a sort that seems very wonderful, nevertheless.

Now, as to the rational of the spirit photograph taken without the aid of the camera. To explain that, I must refer to a phenomenon almost as wonderful, but of which I have had abundant experience. It is possible for the few who not alone can *see* with the astral sense, but can make use of some of the elemental forces belonging to the astral plane, to produce writing on paper without the aid of pen or pencil. This is done sometimes at spiritual *séances* even, and it is not understood in the least by the ordinary spiritualist, but it is done by a process called in occultism "precipitation." On the astral plane thought is a creative power. Your thoughts, if they are sufficiently intense and clear, form images there which are perceptible to others. If you form a thought image of the words you wish to write, and know how to materialise the image by means of etheric matter, you can condense it on paper. Nothing I can say here will enable anyone to *do* the thing, but many things we cannot do ourselves may, nevertheless, be intelligible as do-able by persons adequately gifted. Now, that which seems to take place when a photographic image is produced on a sensitive plate without the aid of a camera is analogous to the precipitation of writing, only the thing precipitated is not visible matter, but a chemical influence. The whole idea is extremely subtle, but there is the accomplished result lying before me, and the solution I have suggested seems the only one available if we want to do something more than gape at it as an inexplicable wonder.

CHAPTER XIV. The Divining Rod.

I HAVE already made some passing allusion to a method by which persons, gifted with a peculiar variety of sensitiveness, are enabled to detect the presence of underground springs of water or metallic ores in a way which baffles the comprehension of the man in the street, and is therefore at once set down by that sapient personage to imposture. I now propose to deal with the subject more fully, and, with this end in view, shall avail myself very freely of the information contained in Professor Barrett's elaborate report on the divining rod addressed to the Society for Psychical Research.

This contains an account of no fewer than 140 cases in which the "Dowsers," as they are called in some parts of the country, have shown that they really have the faculty in question; and I may say at once that, though Professor Barrett set out on his investigation with a distrust of their pretensions, he emerged from that undertaking absolutely convinced that they are genuine exponents of some curious fact in Nature, the science of which he makes no attempt to explain. His inability to do this does not detract in the smallest degree from the value of the evidence he has collected. The stupid, commonplace why of dealing with new experiences is to deny their authenticity if we are not armed beforehand with the means of explaining them. The intelligent plan is to accept facts, however bewildering, and if we are unable at once to explain them, to feel sure they rest on some natural laws of which, as yet, we are ignorant. We should pass them to a scientific suspense account, and wait for later developments of knowledge, instead of presuming to measure the possibilities of Nature by the resources of our limited acquaintance with her laws.

The routine adopted by people who find hidden springs with the help of the divining rod is not calculated to inspire confidence on the part of the ignorant looker-on. The water-finder arms himself with a crooked hazel twig or stick of V-shape, with an end projecting from the apex — a sort of two-plonged fork — and holding a prong in each hand, with the point of the V projecting out in front of him, walks slowly along over the ground to be searched for any hidden springs it may contain. Suddenly he feels an impulse in the stick to point upwards. All that the spectator sees is that he turns the stick upwards, and when the Dowser declares that it turned up of itself without any volition on his part, that same spectator, if he is of the stupid or " O.P." variety, says, " Of course, the Dowser is lying." But the man who wants to know where he should dig his well acts on the advice given, and practically always does find water at the place where the divining rod (in competent hands) has indicated its presence. The geologist smiles with superior wisdom. You get water, he says, by tapping a water-bearing stratum. If you get it by sinking a well at some given spot, you would equally get it by boring anywhere else in the neighbourhood. But the Dowser says,

"You will get it here," and then, going twenty yards away, says, "You will not get it here" — and experience proves him right, in spite of the geologist.

A good many of Professor Barrett' 140 cases illustrate , this very point. It is manifestly impossible, in the compass of such an essay as this, to go into them hi detail. The report lying before me is a closely-printed volume of 280 pages, and anyone wanting to verify my summary of its contents can buy it for himself. There are cases recorded in which the wisdom of the geologist and the instinct of the water-finder have been pitted against each other. The water-finder has said, "Here you will get water!" The geologist has said, "I do not know whether you will or not, but if you do, then you will get it equally anywhere within a radius of twenty or thirty yards." The poor Dowser has indicated places within that radius where no water would be obtained. Wells have been sunk at both places, and the Dowser's predictions have been verified both ways. In one case the well backed by the geologist was constructed with all scientific skill, and it remained almost dry. The other, a mere hole in the ground not nearly so deep, was abundantly filled.

Some of the correspondents who reply to Professor Barrett's inquiries — he collected evidence from all parts of the country, and even from all parts of the empire — describe experiments they have tried with different exponents of the water-finding faculty. First of all, taking one Dowser over their land, they have privately taken note of the spots he indicated as favourable for well-sinking, and have then secured the services of another who knew nothing of the first man's visit. The independent diviners have always "pointed" at the same places, and sometimes a third expert has come to the same conclusions as two unknown predecessors. Some of the professor's "sceptical" correspondents — persons of conventional knowledge and narrow intelligence, who are too often found in the orthodox temples of every science — have, in a lofty spirit of superior wisdom, suggested " tests " to be applied to the " pretended " exponents of the alleged faculty; such as blindfolding them, repeating the trick on a dark night, and so on. The methodical professor points out that among his 140 cases all the suggested tests have actually been applied — the blindfold and the repeating test, for example, cases 2, 6, 17, 25, 45, 73f, 74 and so on with the others. He does not record any apologies tendered by his sceptical correspondents.

I must indulge in a few passing remarks on the use and misuse of the word " scepticism." We should all be sceptics in the sense of being cautious not to believe open-mouthed all we are told. In some departments of orthodoxy scepticism of that sort is specially required. But scepticism properly understood does not mean specific disbelief, any more than Agnosticism properly understood means Atheism. The rational sceptic is the man who, in reference to any particular statement, has not yet had evidence that it is true — he may not care whether the statement is true or false —and then stands outside the subject in question as a professed ignoramus by choice. No one wants to find fault with him if he keeps up that character consistently— even if he should be sceptical as to whether Dickens wrote Pickwick or whether the Cape of Good Hope is south of the Equator. But when a man prides himself on being a sceptic, under the impression that to be so implies greater acumen than is possessed by people who, having looked into the matter in question, have come to definite conclusions, then scepticism is only another name for the foolishness which accompanies unwarrantable conceit; and when a person calls himself a sceptic in reference to any particular question, and, at the same time, takes up the attitude of specific disbelief, then he shows himself an ignoramus in a double sense, as he does not even understand his own language.

The sensitiveness which enables people to use the divining rod with success must not be thought of as confined to a small body of professional experts. There are, it is true, a considerable number of diviners who make their living by the exercise of the faculty, but our painstaking professor shows that the faculty is not confined to any particular age, sex, or class in life. Amongst the successful operators in his long list are to be found a clergyman, a judge, a local manufacturer, a great many ladies, several gardeners, a quaker, a miller, little children, and a French count. As regards the ladies, I have no doubt that in every hundred persons of each sex taken at random, more women than men would be found to possess the faculty, just as we find women of finer sensibility, on the average, than men in almost every department of psychic perception. Perhaps the state of things foreshadows a time in the future when—psychic development having to do with powers as well as with faculties — women will come into possession of a strength against which the muscle of the male will be like that of the ox, a kind of strength entirely under the control of the superior creature! In those days our masculine successors may involuntarily offer up a vicarious atonement for the offence of our tyrannical generation; or it may be that the offenders and the sufferers will be the same entities in reality. But the further discussion of that idea would open out the subject of "Reincarnation" — one of Nature's grandest mysteries— and I must treat that subject with due solemnity by itself.

Professor Barrett, of course, discusses the theory of the divining rod, though, as I have said, he does not come within sight of any intelligible explanation, tike other members of the society he represents, he deserves immense credit for his painstaking accumulation of facts; but he has not studied occultism as a science sufficiently to be guided in the right direction when trying to work out the rationale of such facts. He says, when endeavouring to form some theoretical conclusion: "Few will dispute the proposition that the motion of the forked twig is due to unconscious muscular action. By that he means that the diviner really turns the rod up at the place where water will be found, but does this under the influence of a mysteriously-acquired interior consciousness that the water is there — not because it is guided by his waking mind to do this. On the other hand, conscientiously recognising the significance of some of his own cases, the professor points out that with amateurs like the Rev. J. Blunt, Lady Milbanke, and others, the forked twig not only rotates, but one limb is frequently twisted completely off by the force with which it is driven round and round. Evidently, in such cases, the theory of unconscious muscular action will not work at all. That theory, indeed is little better than a stumbling-block in the path of the Psychic Research Society. It has nothing really to do with the "thought-reading " experiments which, in the volume before me are quoted in support of it.

We shall probably get a little nearer an explanation of the divining rod if we take into account the old-fashioned phenomena which used to be called table-turning before that elementary branch of superphysical experimentation developed into spiritualism. People found that sometimes, when three or four persons sat round a bare table with their hands upon it, it would move about or turn round, though nobody present was playing tricks or pushing. Each person, in such cases, might know that he was honestly abstaining, but he was rarely able to feel sure of the honesty of the others, "the orthodox sceptic" swore that somebody must be pushing, and Faraday even thought he had disposed of the matter by constructing an apparatus to detect pushing; but the tables — indifferent to the annoyance they were giving to the Royal Society — would sometimes move when nobody was even touching them, much less pushing, and then orthodox lookers-on paid no more attention to the problem. They were offended.

For the table-turners themselves, however, gradually becoming spiritualists, the causation at work became partially intelligible. Something was derived from the "medium" — whoever he or she might be — which enabled an invisible being or beings to exert an influence on material object. The tables did not turn "of themselves." They were moved by force of some sort, but it was not the muscular force of the persons seated round — except in cases of cheating, or when idiots among the sitters thought it amusing to play tricks. From those small beginnings all the physical phenomena of spiritualism arose. The invisible beings concerned became more and more competent to bring about startling effects, and the mere movement of heavy objects, without the contact of any human hands whatever, became the child's play of their pursuit. It may still remain difficult to understand every detail of the process; but, for that matter, it is difficult to understand every detail of the process when we light a candle. Is the chemical action that goes on in the wick the cause of the heat, or is the heat the cause of the chemical reaction? A score of mysteries lie further in the background. So with table-turning; but we do know this much — as we also know that by means of a match it is possible to light a candle — granting some ill-understood characteristic in someone present, i.e,, granting the presence of a medium — invisible beings can bring a physical force to bear on material objects.

Now, the plain inference from all this is that its force may be brought to bear upon the hazel twig which causes it to turn under the impulse of invisible beings, when passing over underground water, if the person who holds it is Medium enough to supply the necessary link between the astral and the physical planes of Nature. Is the purpose in view too trumpery or trivial to be worth the attention of an invisible being? If that question is asked, I can only repeat that in the realm of "elemental " agency we have to do with as great a variety of dignity — with a greater variety, really — than that (of a different kind) which we encounter in the physical world as we survey its creatures from the oyster to the man.

CHAPTER XV. Palmistry.

I HAVE referred former chapters to the striking results that have been obtained in some cases by the practice of palmistry. The subject is before the world so frequently in these days, that it seems desirable to discuss it rather more fully before passing on to more exalted themes. I do not propose to add one more to the numerous manuals of palmistry available for the use of those who wish to become practical palmists, but I want to indicate what kind of knowledge concerning a person's health, character, and destiny can really be obtained by the study of the lines on the hand, and where all possibilities of that sort stop short.

The success of palmistry in attracting attention out of all proportion to its real importance as a branch of occult science is obviously due to the fact that almost everybody has a pair of hands, and quite everybody is interested in all that directly concerns him or herself. People who loftily affect to regard the whole thing as utter nonsense are eager, none the less, to put out a hand whenever opportunity offers, and have their "fortunes told," if only "for the fun off the thing," with mental reservations to the effect that the palmists are sometimes right by accident when they read in the hand that the possessor is remarkable for courage, generosity, and truthfulness, or for amiability, sweetness of temper, and unselfishness, according to self. In all ranks of life people grasp openly or surreptitiously at every chance of having their hands read, flocking to Bond Street for the purpose, or getting a consultation down the area for sixpence, as their station in the world may dictate.

The contrast between the actual practice of the present age and its conventional pretences is amusing in a high degree, but it is true, though in a sense very different from that in which the phrase is often used, that ignorance and superstition go hand in hand. Ignorance of the facts to which Nature's mysteries give rise to the silliest kind of superstition possible — that which makes the exponents of such ignorance believe in their own sagacity, in the ages of faith, no doubt, many beliefs prevailed which were superstitious in the common acceptation of the word, but a great many other beliefs that would now be classed as superstitious were really empirical conclusions from experience, and representative of a much sounder state of mind than that of the man who is vain enough to suppose that nothing can be true that fails to chime in with the' knowledge, such as it is, that; he happens to possess.

Palmistry is neither a system of chicanery and imposture nor a sure and certain method of divining the future. But every rational being who seriously looks into the matter will find that, beyond all dispute or uncertainty, some broad correspondences are to be traced between the shape and markings of the hand and the character, health, and general prosperity, or the reverse, of the person whose hand is considered. This ought not to be surprising from the point of view of anyone who has even a dim appreciation of the harmony that pervades Nature. Who is there who would not recognise some kinds of correspondence between character and external form? You see a man with a big square jaw and a well-Get-forward chin, and you instinctively feel that such a man has a certain force of character (whether it is a good or a bad force is quite another matter). If you are in presence of two men, one of whom has a high, broad forehead, and the other a head that slopes back directly , above the eyebrows, and you are told, " One of them is a literary or scientific genius, and the other rather a commonplace goose," would anybody of the least experience of life have a moment's hesitation in saying which was which? " Ah!" it may be answered, " that is because the brain has to do with mental capacity; the hand has nothing to do with it."

Be that so, or not more likely that we have not yet identified the harmony of Nature in respect of soul characteristics and the physique generally? '

It is just as contrary to common sense as to the more precise teachings of occult science to suppose that the human soul in a body is like a doll in a box, the doll and the box having been made by different artificers without reference to one another. The materialistic view, as completely as the higher one, will suggest that the body and the soul are intimately related all through. The materialist would argue that the soul is the product of the body, and the occultist that the body is the product of the soul (in a roundabout way), but both regard the two as interdependent. And just because Nature always does her work so thoroughly, the reasonable inference is that every part of the body has some correspondence (if only we could detect it) with some attribute of the real entity, which it expresses on this plane of life. Nothing is more probable than that the hand — so variable in its attributes, comparing one hand with another — should be conspicuously related to interior soul characteristics.

Then we turn to experience. If, in any department of life, we find that a certain effect follows a certain cause, in ninety-nine cases out of every hundred, even if we cannot say why it should, nobody of reasonable mind would refuse to recognise a connection between such cause and effect. Granting the presence of their cause, he would say it is about a hundred to one that such results will follow. That is the situation, pretty nearly, with the broadest and most elementary deductions of palmistry. You will rarely, if ever, find a mature person, who has enjoyed good health all life through, without a clean, well-defined line running round the base of the thumb. I do not know why that should be so, any more than I know why certain wave lengths of light give rise to certain colour sensations in my consciousness, but I know they always do. So with any very old person. You will seldom or never find such a person without a long line round the base of the thumb curving round towards the wrist, even if it be broken in places or crossed with various markings. So, when a palmist sees a long "life-line," as it is called, on a young person's hand, he says, "The great probability is you will have a long life," and if the line is very clean and free from certain markings, he will add, with equal confidence, "You will have a very healthy life." Again, you will seldom or never make mistakes with the line which in all hands begins at the top of the life-line or near it, and goes, or tends to go, across the hand.

In persons below the general level of intelligence that line will be short; in persons of conspicuous ability it will be well-defined and long. In a young person some broad conclusions may be derived from the consideration of that line which will rarely mislead the observer.

Above this line there is generally one which crosses the hand underneath the little mounds at the root of the fingers, and this is called the"" heart line." The 'indications it gives are nearly as precise as those of the other two, and the line which sometimes runs up the middle of the hand from the wrist to the root of the middle finger (and is called the Saturnian) is very significant when clearly defined, but not often found in perfectly good order. That line has to do with the "fate," or destiny in life, and the reading of it is rendered difficult by a multitude of complications that will be found duly set forth in the various manuals of palmistry. Broadly, however, it may be affirmed that the hand of any old person who has had a brilliant, unbroken, continuous career in life, will be found to have a fairly well-defined Saturnian line; while those whose life has been troubled, irregular, unsuccessful in the sphere to which they belong), will be found without any such continuous line. The interpretation to be assigned to its breakings or crossmarkings will be given in some of the books one way, and in some another, but there is such a general correspondence in the experience of different students, that we cannot remain in doubt as to the broad fact that — for unfathomable reasons — there is a correspondence between the line in question and the character of the person's life. I have to recognise that, in talking of the " character " of a life, I am using the word in a sense very unlike that implied when we talk of the character of the person himself. For the mere materialist the life is a succession of events, the general character of which can be talked of when they are over, but in reference to which it unconceivable that they can have any character one way or the other before they occur. Therein lies the materialist's blunder, but to discuss it fully would carry us into the depths of metaphysics. Meanwhile for the purposes of palmistry, it is not necessary to be metaphysical; merely to observe facts is enough, 'and the palmist argues, " People who have gone through such and such lives will always be found to have had hands marked, as regards the Saturnian, in such and such a way." Therefore, when he sees a young person's hand marked in such and such a way, he says, "That person will have such and such a life." The prediction has no origin in any train of reasoning, but practice shows that in the majority of cases it turns out right.

The more minute predictions of palmistry are all derived from patient observation of innumerable cases. This study, be it remembered, is no affair of yesterday. It has been going on for ages, and while no writer on the subject has ever dreamed of penetrating the mystery involved to the extent of saying why this or that characteristic or event w life should produce this or that line in a hand, the palmists of all generations have been free from the foolish habit of denying facts, merely because they could not understand their rationale. One of my oldest books on the subject is dated 1671, and is described on the title page as "by Richard Saunders, student in Astrology and Physic," and the imprint tells us, in the quaint language of the time, that the book is "printed by H. Bragis, for Nathaniel Brook, at the sign of the Angel in Cornhill, and at his shop at the east end of the Royal Exchange." Old Saunders is generally regarded by modern palm lists as an authority to be greatly reverenced. Besides his general account of the significance to be attached to the main lines of the hand, the author proceeds to furnish us with a long series of diagrams, showing all sorts of unusual lines that may be encountered in some cases, and appends an account of what they mean. Por example, certain lines " signify a man to be the cause of shedding his own blood with manifest peril of life." Another line " signifies a man shall inhabit out of his natural country, and shall die there, and by how much «the greater they are found in the beginning the sooner, and the bigger they are in the end, so much the longer ere he die." In another case the signification is "hurt from four-footed beasts." In another, drunken bestial condition." The palmists of Saunders's time were not, it would seem, so bent as his modern successors on finding complimentary meanings for the lines they examined. Indeed, the book before me is so very plain-spoken about the meaning of certain marks, that decorum forbids their quotation.

To be a competent palmist, a student must be saturated with a knowledge of all these purely empirical readings, and must have the faculty of balancing one against another. And it stands to reason that, in regard to the meaning of marks that only rarely occur, there cannot be so broad a foundation of observations to base upon as in the case of the lines, which everybody has in one condition or another. Then, again, the determination, according to the rules of palmistry, of the time at which certain events marked in the hand as impending will actually come off is very difficult.

On the life-line, if the indications in question are illnesses, time has to be reckoned from the top of the line downwards towards the wrist — the whole line representing the entire life, and portions of it corresponding fractions. On the Saturnian, many events affecting the career are to be recorded, the bottom of the line is the beginning, and the top, near the fingers, the latter period. Assuredly, there is "no sense" in such reckonings; only people 'ho meekly accept the experience of ages, and have thoroughly imbibed all the accumulated records thereof, can read a hand and make predictions that turn out right in a proportion of cases, putting 'he theory of coincidence entirely out of court.

So far, I have dealt only with the kind of palmistry which anybody may learn to practise if he has the patience to study the books, and the capacity to keep their variegated contents in his mind. To do that is to accomplish a' task far greater than learning a foreign language. But, after it is done, nobody will be really a first-fate palmist without a considerable infusion of the clairvoyant faculty. The significations of the markings to be examined in a hand are so extremely complex, that it is hardly possible for anyone to interpret and balance them all correctly. But as a palmist with some clairvoyant faculty pores over his task, he gets impressions that prompt him to look for corresponding signs in the hand, and then he finds them, though otherwise it is almost certain that they would have escaped his attention.

I have left myself no room in which to discuss the contemptible imbecility of the present law affecting the practice of palmistry, but on that subject anyone who has finalised these explanations with any appreciation of the sound natural truths that underlie them, will be able to form his own conclusions.

CHAPTER XVI. Occult Powers.

It is immensely important for anyone who wants to obtain a clear insight into the variegated subjects with which I have been dealing, to draw a sharp distinction between occult faculties and occult powers. Especially is it necessary to do this when we are talking of spiritualistic mediumship. One often hears people use the phrase, "a powerful medium," in reference to one in whose presence great and remarkable phenomena take place. To do the mediums themselves no more than justice; they rarely fall into the use of such mistaken language themselves, for they always emphasise the theory that all phenomena are brought about by the " power " of the spirits, they themselves being quite passive in the matter. In connection with Mesmerism, on the other hand, it is not a misuse of language to talk of a powerful mesmerist, because there is an almost infinite range of possibility in that direction, and because the results of mesmerism, if it be genuine, are brought about by an energy emanating from the mesmerist. But nine times out of ten, or in a much larger proportion, when people talk of a powerful mesmerist, they are confusing the share in the result due to his energy with that due to the sensitiveness of his patient. The truth is, that very few modern mesmerists of the kind generally met with about the world at large have any power much worth speaking of. They may all have some trace of such power, and the rest depends on the varying degrees of sensitiveness of the people they practise upon.

The distinction is very clear when once apprehended. The analogies of ordinary life make it intelligible. Sight and hearing are faculties obviously, not powers; muscular energy is a power, not a faculty. Going behind the scenes a little, the consciousness that is impressed by the senses of sight or hearing is a faculty; the will which brings the muscles into play is a power. Now, when we are investigating the mysteries of Nature, we are, for the most part availing ourselves of faculties, existent either in ourselves or others, by which facts can be cognised that would not be perceptible to senses of the ordinary sort. But when we come in contact with occurrences of an abnormal kind, such as those continually met with in connection with spiritualism, then obviously we are in the presence of powers exercised by some person or persons either in the flesh or belonging to some other " plane " of Nature.

In the case of the spiritualistic séance, we are merely dealing, as far as externals go, with people, all of whom — medium included — are quite passive. The power exercised must, therefore, emanate from another plane. But at once we see that there is nothing unusual or extraordinary in that

Power, which generally does emanate, when you come to think of it, from another plane. Throw a cricket ball, and what has really happened? The ball is impelled by your arm, but what causes your arm to move? Your will, which is really a force belonging to the spiritual side of your nature. It belongs to another plane. And though the truth of the matter gets disguised in the mask of the commonplace, the mysterious force of will is constantly acting on otherwise inert matter to produce effects. The muscles are not alive in themselves. They do not act without the impulse of a force from another plane in any one of the thousands of movements they make every day.

But can the will control any other sort of matter besides the muscles and the other activities of the body? In all the experience of spiritualism the volition exercised comes from beings on another plane of Nature, and the passive spectators get into the habit of thinking that, while "the spirits" can do almost anything, spirits still in the body — ordinary living people, that is to say— can do nothing in the way, for instance, of controlling physical matter, except by means of the muscles. It's the great failing of spiritualists, as a body, that they will not take the trouble to reason about the phenomena they are constantly observing. By their own hypothesis, the movement of physical objects, and the still more wonderful passage of matter through matter — of a blade of dry grass through a table, for example, which a friend of mine has seen accomplished in the light — is accomplished by spirits who were once ordinary human beings like themselves. Why is it that A., B., or C., who could not make even a magnetic needle alter its' position by his mere will in life, is no sooner " dead " than he can work miracles in the way of causing heavy objects to move without the contact of physical muscles?

In a vague sort of way the lookers-on assume that in "spirit-land" he has learned to do things he could not do in life, which, in a certain sense, is true enough; but the answer only restates the question, What is it that he has learned? Now, the first statement I have to make in reply to the question. Why cannot people still in the flesh move physical objects by their mere will without touching them? is that the question does not fit the facts. Some people can!

The capacity to do this is enormously rarer than the attribute which renders some people mediums — in a condition to surrender to "the spirits some of the invisible constituents of their own organism which have to be made use of in accomplishing results that ordinary people might call magical. Certainly, such people have acquired their powers by the exercise, in the first instance, of a faculty.

They are necessarily people who have the clairvoyant faculty which enables them to cognise the potentialities of the astral plane, by which alone they can manipulate the forces which, in connection with such undertakings, they want to bring into play.

Coming at once to concrete illustrations; I will describe some of the simplest of such achievement that first attracted my own attention to the stupendous problems of occult science. It is more than twenty years ago now since I first made the acquaintance of a very remarkable person, who has been the subject of more complicated misunderstandings all round and in both, directions than anybody who has ever lived before, I should think—the late Mme. Blavatsky. I had previously seen a good deal of spiritualism, and was familiar with many such phenomena as I have been talking about in this book, but I had obtained no intellectual satisfaction along that road, beyond the immensely important assurance of continued life after death, and I had not contemplated the possibility of powers analogous to those exercised by " the spirits " as being within the grasp of people still in the flesh. But, from the first day of my acquaintance with her, though herself restrained at that time by embarrassments afterwards removed, she made it clear to me that her will could influence physical matter.

The simplest evidence of that state of things had to do with the production by her, at will, of the sounds known as spirit-rapping. The stupid argument of the disbeliever in old days used to be: How can a sound, which is a mechanical vibration of the atmosphere, be set up by any non-mechanical intangible agency? We who knew that the thing occurred could not say how it was brought about; only we knew it did happen, and we also thought we knew that the unintelligible result required the co-operation of some being out of the body. This idea Mme. Blavatsky showed me to be a mistake. She could make those sounds occur at any time or place without moving a muscle. I was enabled to test this capacity of hers scores of times, in all the ways I could think of. To detail the circumstances of this investigation would take up too much time now.

They are all minutely described in a book I wrote a year or two later, when the experiments in question had been eclipsed by a great many others of enormously more important significance. That book was called The Occult world, and therein the subject I am now dealing with can be studied more at length. And here let me remark that the long series of wonderful phenomena described, of a kind wholly unlike those of spiritualism — in that they were the product of embodied human will — have never been shaken, even as regards their evidential value, in any of the storms that have since raged round Mme. Blavatsky's name.

Other and wholly different phenomena, with which I have had nothing to do, have been challenged as regards their authenticity; but I can afford to pass all that by with absolute indifference. A certain famous inquiry, conducted with a stupidity that was itself phenomenal, and of which the results were swallowed by the Society for Psychical Research with a gullibility to match, has left uncritical bystander' under the impression that somehow Mme Blavatsky's wonder-working has been exposed. Not only is that not the fact, but the most important wonder-working with which Mme. Blavatsky was ever concerned — that which is described in The Occult World — has never even been seriously attacked. Ridiculed? Yes; but, given and adequately grovelling wit, and anything in heaven or earth can be ridiculed. My statements of fact have never been seriously challenged, and as for the inferences to which they lead, these can be drawn as reasonably to-day as twenty years ago.

Summed up briery, those inferences are that, granting an adequate faculty of clairvoyance on the astral plane, so that you can study the nature of the forces available there, and see what you are doing, you — that is to say, a qualified human being still in the flesh — can exercise powers over matter belonging to the order that used to be thought magical. It is, for example, within the power of such persons to accomplish such feats as I have described in talking of spiritualism — to disintegrate physical objects, transport them to a distance, and reintegrate them' there, so that, in effect, a person possessing this power could possess himself practically of anything he coveted — the gold in the cellars of the Bank of England, for example — without stirring out of his arm-chair at home.

And having given that rather full-flavoured illustration of what occult power might "enable a man to accomplish, it may begin to dawn upon the minds of my readers why the Authority that rules the world should, at the present stage of human evolution, and in the present condition of human morals, think fit to put some impediments in the way of the acquisition of occult powers. If they were easily acquirable, the social life of modern communities would be thrown into ghastly confusion; for life, as well as property, would be insecure, — the power which, employed in one way to disintegrate matter, could just as readily be turned to the commission of murders, which Sherlock Holmes himself would be no more competent to detect than to find out who might be responsible for an earthquake in Japan. The curious part of the story is, that the total eclipse and disappearance out of the ordinary world of all traces of occult power only dates back to the beginning of the very advanced civilisation of which at present we are so justly proud. In the dismal middle ages some remnants of occult power actually lingered in the ordinary world, handed down from remoter civilisations — indeed, from that Atlantean civilisation of which I wrote in one of the earlier chapters of this book, in the faded and ignoble shape known as "witchcraft." The comical prigs of current culture think witchcraft was all nonsense because they cannot now reproduce it. And yet Lecky admits that the evidence for the reality of witchcraft is overwhelming. He, indeed, adduces the absurd conclusion that this shows the fallibility of human testimony. It is proved, as far as testimony goes, that Witchcraft existed, but we know that it is inconsistent with "the known laws of Nature" So everybody concerned must have been a victim of hallucination or telling lies! No funnier phrase has ever been coined for the amusement of those who can see beyond the aspects of Nature unveiled the senses, than that delightful expression about her " known laws " that I have more than once had occasion to quote.

The safeguard of humanity from the premature diffusion of occult powers is to be found in the fact that, under the operation of laws as difficult to disregard as those belonging to the known order, no one, at the present state of evolution, can obtain the knowledge which invests anyone still in the flesh with those powers, unless he has given assurances that cannot be misunderstood either by himself or the higher authorities concerned, to the effect that he is morally incapable of using such powers for evil or for merely selfish purposes. The reader must be referred to the literature of modern occultism if he wishes that statement elaborated more fully, but the main idea I am anxious to leave on his mind for the moment is the distinction with which I began between faculties and powers, and the corresponding distinction between spiritualism and occultism. I do not want to run down or decry the interest, and for many people the great value, of spiritualism as a pursuit, but it leads merely, and by the hypothesis only lead, to personal familiarity with some of the phenomena of the astral plane, or, in rare cases to some familiarity with the conditions of existence on higher planes. Occultism, on the other hand, aims at the acquisition of such interior conditions and knowledge as may promote the growth, within the man himself, of conditions bringing with them occult power. And yet the power is not the object of pursuit Is that a paradox? At all events, it is not a very difficult riddle to read. The powers come as the consequence of a certain advanced condition of spiritual evolution, and with them come into consciousness a higher set of motives for action than any related to the physical plane of life. Then a spiritualised science begins to merge into a scientific religion, and horizons widen before the mind in all directions.

CHAPTER XVII. The Purposes of Occult Study.

The. study of all the manifold varieties of natural mystery with which these essays have been concerned would still be interesting even if we remained, at the end, blankly wondering at the strange energies working behind the scenes but, happily, that study leads to a great deal more than the vague conviction expressed by the familiar phrase that recognises more in heaven and earth than is dreamed of in commonplace philosophy. Certainly that acknowledgment is the first step towards the better understanding of our place in Nature, and hence the importance of getting people to realise the genuine character many abnormal phenomena. Nineteenth-century science has been unfavourable to the appreciation of such phenomena, and no true occultist complains of this, because the growth of that science has been supremely important in educating the human mind to think with exactitude. But now that a new era has begun, the mental powers thus acquired must be turned to other aspects of Nature, besides those which have to do merely with the forces of the physical plane. From the study of superphysical mysteries, when these have once fairly forced themselves on the attention, the highly- trained faculties of the mind — evolved by the exercises of the nineteenth century — will discover amongst these mysteries the clue to the comprehension, not merely of much that has hitherto seemed inexplicable, but also of the deeper mystery which lies in the background — the scheme of natural law which regulates the development of the human mind itself.

Nothing is more persistently forced upon our thoughts, as we observe the phenomena of the higher spiritualism, of the mesmeric trance, of sensitiveness to psychic impression of all kinds, or as we weigh the evidence of those persons able to cognise places and people at a distance from their sleeping bodies, than the broad fact that consciousness is not — as some materialists of the past century would endeavour to maintain — a function of the physical brain. All who have had the opportunity of observing the beautiful processes of mesmeric clairvoyance will appreciate the fundamental truth that human consciousness must have its seat in something that is distinctly separable from the body, not only when death puts an end to the activities of the brain altogether, but during life as well. During waking life, indeed, the brain is in intimate relationship with the thinking faculty, but it must be regarded as an instrument on which the real thinker is playing — not as the thinker itself.

Every religion that has talked about the soul has vaguely implied this, but most people who seek to understand a statement before they grant it their belief are discontented with the idea of a disembodied consciousness which has, so to speak, no vehicle in which to dwell. Occult science comes to their relief. It has discovered other orders of matter besides those that can be seen and touched by the physical mechanism of the body, and it has become familiar with the fact that every human being is furnished by Nature with vehicles of consciousness, or bodies constructed of these higher orders of matter. To the appropriate senses of people more completely developed than most of us, these higher vehicles are fully visible, and it is in them, not in the physical body, that consciousness truly resides.

During the waking state these higher vehicles are intimately blended with the vehicle or body specially appropriate to this plane of existence. Indeed, it is just this blending that constitutes the waking state. Perhaps anyone approaching the consideration of such thoughts as these for the first time, will suppose that it is only in the case of abnormally-gifted people that the higher vehicles of consciousness can take flight from the body without danger to life, and return to it from distant wanderings. The truth is, that every human being quits his body during sleep. Getting out of it is the act of going to sleep, though physiologists have quite accurately detected some physical changes that take place concurrently in the brain, and have erroneously fancied that these changes constitute sleep. It will be convenient to use a technical term here, and to concentrate our attention on the vehicle of consciousness which it describes, therefore we will talk of that in which the consciousness of every human being in sleep goes "out of the body as " the astral body."

People may ask how it is that we do not all remember our flights in the astral body, as some gifted persons appear to do. The occultist is not at all embarrassed by that question, any more than the gymnast would be puzzled if asked why one person can climb a rope hand over hand, while another could hardly support his weight that way. The muscles of the one are better developed than those of the other. The higher vehicles of man are the product of evolution like the physical frame, and they are of much slower growth. The race is very far, as yet, from having reached perfection of form- even on the physical plane — though the ground plan of the perfect physical form has by this time been fairly well sketched out — but the higher vehicles are not nearly so far advanced, except in a few cases (few, that is to say, in relation to the enormous population of the earth). Everyone who understands the matter can do a great deal to stimulate their growth —

indeed, it would hardly be an exaggeration to say that they can only grow when people understand the matter, and set themselves to help the evolutionary law — but at present, as the race has been developed so far, the astral body is not much more competent to enjoy and work with the opportunities of the sphere of Nature in which it exists, than the physical body of a baby in arms would be able to make use of the gymnast's appliances.

At one stage or another of all such inquiry, people will be sure to feel that it is all very unfair on those who are born amongst the undeveloped majority — not provided the law of evolution or Providence — whichever phrase we like to employ — with astral bodies capable of conscious flights through higher regions of Nature. Why are we set to accomplish our little run through earthly existence at a period of the world's growth, when it seems we are not half able to enjoy the opportunities this same world will offer to our more richly-endowed successors? This cry is only, in another form, the same that has so often arisen from the hardly-used bulk of humanity in reference to the inequalities of well-being amongst the children of men on the physical plane. Is it not terribly unfair that one should be born rich and another poor, one healthy and another diseased, one in the midst of conditions that lead to a life of honour and distinction, another in surroundings that conduce as surely to a life of crime and penal treatment? The question brings us to the very heart of the magnificent spiritual discoveries which the study of occult mystery has unveiled for our reverence, our admiration, and our consolation in this world of trial and suffering.

For less teachable generations than our own, religion has answered these pitiful appeals by giving assurances that somehow, in another world, all such apparent injustice would be remedied. There poor and the downtrodden will be compensated by boundless happiness; there the rich man will be denied entrance to "the kingdom of Heaven." Somctimes the rich man has objected that this system would be as unfair as the other, if he is to be kept "eternally " in an inferior state hereafter merely becausc hc has had a better time than his neighbours for a few years on earth; but, meanwhile, he has consoled himself by never really believing the story, whilc the sufferer has clung to one half of it, at all events, with touching fidelity. And, in truth, the occultist does not want to dispute the broad principle that, in states of spiritual happiness succeeding this life and enduring for very long periods of time, the victims of the world's inequality will find such ample compensation for temporary hardships that these will seem very unimportant in the retrospect. Occultism, in reference to heaven, merely puts a definite complexion on the condition of the after life rendering states of existence, which were unintelligible before, plainly harmonious with a scientific view of Nature.

But it does a great deal more than this. It shows us that, even on this earth, in the long run, justice will be vindicated in every case, for every man and woman now living is merely going through one phase of Earthly existence. He or she will come back again and live here again, and then again and again through a long vista or series of lives; always the same soul, the same centre of consciousness in all the different bodies it may come to inhabit as the ages advance. Will it not be seen how the mind is prepared to comprehend this idea by the fact, already discussed, that the soul, the consciousness which is the man in any given life, is not a function of the body going on at the time, but something quite separable from and independent thereof?

Nothing worth keeping is destroyed when the one life ends. The person dying — as hundreds of observations by those who can range the astral plane show — is very often unable to realise that he is dead. He feels just the same as before, until he gradually begins to perceive that he has come into possession of new faculties that he did not possess before. He is simply on the threshold of a new life, and the experiences of that are variegated and prolonged beyond anything that ordinary imagination is likely to suggest. But, eventually, after ages have elapsed, the man, so to speak, dies out of the spiritual condition, and become once more immersed in a vehicle of physical plane consciousness — that is to say, he is born again on earth, it may be in quite different surroundings from those of his last life, and passes through another phase of earthly existence.

The profound truth, which, on reflection,' will be seen at one stroke to answer most of the riddles of the painful earth, is known to occultism as the Doctrine of Reincarnation. It has been explained by theosophical writers, myself among the number, over and over again, with full detail, during the last twenty years, but it is difficult to eradicate some misconceptions on the subject from the public mind. Thick-headed people, like a blunderer who fancies himself a critic of oriental ideas, in a volume, mainly of rubbish, called *Asia and Europe,* scoff at the reincarnation idea, because they say it is impossible to imagine human beings becoming animals. Every writer on reincarnation has carefully explained that the old-world notion called " transmigration," which embodied the idea of a relapse to animal incarnations, was the mere caricature of the true doctrine, put out by people who had not fully grasped it in ancient times, or found themselves constrained to disguise it. The law of reincarnation is not a provision for backsliding on the scale of creation, but, on the contrary, for progressive evolution. Every new life is a new opportunity for the soul, or "Ego," as we sometimes say, to advance his own moral and intellectual development, and it is, to all intents and purposes, through the efforts of such lives alone that advance is possible. But without going fully into that branch of the subject — for I can do no more at present than sketch the outlines of the great truth — it is important to recognize that, though there can be no retrogression in successive rebirths as regards the kingdoms of Mature — once a man always a man, till, in some inconceivably distant future, something better still may be possible — at the same time, the environment or surroundings of each life in turn must be the accurate expression of the soul's desert.

According to the way in which the opportunities, whatever they were, whether great or small, of the previous life' were availed of, 'so is the character of the next life defined. In rough language, everyone gets, in his or her next life, just the sort of treatment that he or she has deserved by action in the previous life, and this is the way in which the law of reincarnation, with its sublime companion law, which determines the circumstances of each new incarnation — the law of Karma, as it is technically called — provides for the perfectly fair treatment, in the long run, of every member of the human family.

To avoid the continual use of a double pronoun, let us call the soul "it." Its station in life each time it reappears on earth, its bodily health, the happiness or unhappiness it encounters in its relationship with other incarnate souls, are all result of its Karma or action in the last or other by-gone lives. And be it remembered always that different souls are of all imaginably different ages. Some of those around us, as we walk through a London street, have begun their career as human beings millions of years before others; and, to the eye of the occultist, the great masses of the poorer population — with a very minute percentage of exceptions due to peculiar Karma — are the younger members of the human family, doing, for a time, its rougher work. We have all been through the same mill in by-gone ages, even if we are promoted to other sorts of work in the current life, and for, all who are honestly and courageously doing whatever work has been set for them this time by Nature's decree, promotion is as certain in the future as the growth of a healthy seedling into a plant.

Another point of immense interest to be remembered is that, in the long run, the soul has an equal experience of both sexes. Complexities of the law, which it is impossible to go into here, determine in each case, as it is entering on a new life, whether that shall be a male or a female life. But let it not be supposed for one instant that the one is superior to the other as an opportunity of accomplishing evolutionary growth. Both kinds must be experienced by the soul, in order that it may be prepared for ulterior destinies of perfection.

Leaving the immensely important thoughts that have been developed in the last few paragraphs to germinate in the minds of my readers, I must now, for the present at all events, say good-bye to them, very sure that in many cases I must have started them on lines of investigation and discovery that will do them more good, in the long run, than as yet they foresee. The advance guard of the human race in civilised lands stands really at a critical period of evolution, and the grand results of the future depend for each of us, in turn, on the extent to which we come into conscious relationship with the answers to those riddles which Nature's Mysteries present for the education of the higher faculties of mankind.

THE END

Made in the USA
Columbia, SC
23 December 2024

50491825R00059